PICKLEBALL!

The Curious History of Pickleball

Plus Recipes from the ORIGINAL KITCHEN for the Perfect PICKLEBALL PARTY!

FROM ITS ORIGINS AS PICKLEPONG
1959-1963

PATRICK W. SMITH

YellowBird Publishing Ventures

Published in the United States by YellowBird Ventures, LLC.
All Rights Reserved. No part of this book may be reproduced in any form, or by any electronic or mechanical means, including information storage and retrieval systems without written permission from the publisher. To obtain special reproduction permission for Reviews and Articles, please contact us at this email address: **yellowbirdinformation@gmail.com**

YellowBird Ventures, LLC
Guilford, Connecticut 06437
Author: Patrick W. Smith
Editor: Maria Mortali
Cover Design: Book Designers.com, San Francisco, CA
Illustrations: YBPV
First Edition

Title: **PICKLEBALL!**
The Curious History of Pickleball From its Origins as Picklepong 1959 - 1963

1. Nonfiction 2. Paddle Sports / Pickleball 3. Sports Humor / Essays 4. Recipes Food / Hors D'oeuvres / Entertaining
5. Recipes Alcoholic Beverages / Bartending & Cocktails 6. History / Local & State / Pacific Northwest (OR, WA) / United States

Print ISBN: **979-8-9875408-0-0**
EBook ISBN: **979-8-9875408-1-7**
Audio Book ISBN: **979-8-9875408-2-4**
PCN: **NRC110597**
Library of Congress Control Number **(LCCN): 2023901375**

Publisher's Cataloging-in-Publication Data
provided by Five Rainbows Cataloging Services

Names: Smith, Patrick W., author.
Title: Pickleball! : the curious history of pickleball from its origins as picklepong 1959-1963 / Patrick W. Smith.
Description: Guilford, CT : YellowBird Publishing Ventures, 2023.
Identifiers: LCCN 2023901375 (print) | ISBN 979-8-9875408-0-0 (paperback) | ISBN 979-8-9875408-1-7 (ebook) | ISBN 979-8-9875408-2-4 (audiobook)
Subjects: LCSH: Pickleball (Game) | Pickleball (Game)--History. | Racket games. | Entertaining. | Recipes. | BISAC: SPORTS & RECREATION / Racket Sports / Pickleball. | SPORTS & RECREATION / Essays. | COOKING / Beverages / Alcoholic / Bartending & Cocktails. | COOKING / Entertaining.
Classification: LCC GV990 .S65 2023 (print) | LCC GV990 .S65 2023 (ebook) | DDC 796.34--dc23.

© • YellowBird Publishing Ventures® • 2022

Dedication

Dear Reader,

Whether you are a Pickleballing Pro, an Up and Comer, or a Hopeful Wanna-be, I invite you to enjoy the story of the birth of the original game from one of the last remaining eyewitnesses to its genesis.

This is a Story of The Birth of Pickleball – BEFORE 1965!

The tale of the life and times of the early Pickled-Pioneers who unwittingly influenced Joel Pritchard and his tribe before the game as we now know it was even a glimmer in anyone's eye.

In addition, an enticing gastronomy of authentic recipes awaits you at the end to help you create your own Perfect Pickleball Party.

Dedicated To My Long-Passed Family on Whidbey Island, along with The Pritchard Family on Bainbridge, William Bell, Barney McCallum and their clans, and My Frye Island, Maine Pickle-Balling Pals who reminded me of the *Happy Place* from whence I came.

~ Patrick Smith
Guilford, Connecticut

Five minutes from the Courts on Frye Island
Lake Sebago, Maine

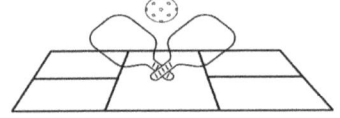

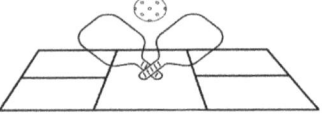

Table of Contents

Dedication	i
Table of Contents	iii
Preface	iv

~ BACK IN THE DAY ~

In the Beginning ...	1
1963	5
A Gherkin By Any Other Name, Would Taste As Sweet	8
The Lay of the Land	11
North by Northwest Pickleball at Ground Zero	15
Local Color ~ Then and Now	19
Itinerary Ad Libitum ~ The Same Old, Same Old	23
Preparation of the Pitch	29
The Necessary Accoutrements	33
The Playbill	37
Let The Games Begin	39

~ WHERE WE ARE NOW ~

Pickleball Now ~ It's Just Competitive Enough	45
Our Sensational Conflation Nation	47
Sphairistike to Tennis to Pickleball	51
The Sound ~ Unique	53
Closing	55
Afterword	56

~ WELCOME TO THE KITCHEN ~

Gretchen's Gherkins	57
Lugubrious Lubricating Libations	59
PAT'S PERFECT PICKLEBALL PARTY PLANNER ~ RECIPES FOR A PICKLED ~ BALL	67

~ INQUIRING MINDS ~

Appendix 1 Chief Seattle's Speech and Letter ...	85
Appendix 2 Pickleball Terminology	95
About The Author	103
Credits and Acknowledgements	107

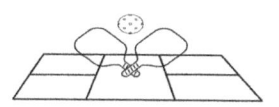

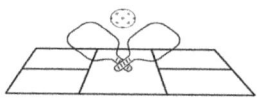

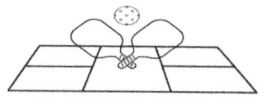

Preface

Like most things creative, the genesis of Pickleball comes with its own fragmented and lumpy baggage. Not unlike the *Telephone Game*, every telling of its tangential story changes the original in some small but fundamental fashion.

It is abundantly and inarguably clear that Mr. Joel Pritchard, Mr. Barney McCallum, Mr. William Bell, and a collection of their friends were the catalyst that launched Pickleball on a trajectory that brought it to us today, codifying and formalizing its rules and regulations into the game we now love to play.

My purpose here is not to challenge the veracity of the well-documented history of these facts. My purpose is instead to bring to light the angular backstory, the unmarked trail preceding Pickleball's earliest development and the two "political" friends of the Pritchards who are sadly, but not surprisingly, missing from that early list of influential contributors. They are absent, not because of intentional omission, but because they lived on the next island to the north and shared a friendship with the Pritchards that was far more professional than personal. They are my aunt and uncle, Gretchen and Charles "Chuck" Bechtell of Whidbey Island, fundraisers for many and various republican causes politic. Not only are they my family, but also they are the actual progenitors of the game that was later formalized and popularized by our neighbors to the south, the Pritchards of Bainbridge Island.

I now, humbly, offer you this account of the earlier pre-history of Pickleball, pre-Pritchard, primarily to grant belated and posthumous credit where it is at last due, to the "Inventors" Bechtell. My labors are purely for your entertainment and edification, simply because I think it will be at the very least an interesting account for you to ponder. The long untold backstory, the remarkable and somewhat blemished birth story of Pickleball, set in the *slantendicular* environment that spawned its creation before its official birthdate of 1965.

Here then, dear reader, is my happy firsthand account, an up-close and personal look at the original Pickleballers in their native habitat – retrograde from 1963, from the crystal-clear memories of an actual eyewitness, albeit a young one.

*Ten minutes from the Courts
Guilford, Connecticut*

One
~ BACK IN THE DAY ~

In the Beginning ...

My childhood home on Mercer Island stood behind the trees on the right, before the new I-90 bridge was built connecting the USA from Seattle to Boston.

In 1956, the happy occasion of a child's birth took place in Seattle: mine.

At age three, living with my single mother on Mercer Island, smack dab in the middle of Lake Washington east of Seattle, I began a seasonal sojourn with my father John to the summer home of his sister and brother-in-law, the unwitting progenitors of Pickleball. Father John and I would repair to scenic Whidbey Island in the "Salish Sea" of Washington State's Puget Sound to visit and vacation with the Bechtells, my paternal side of King County's branch of the collective family Smith.

I delighted in long weekends observing my father's birth family and absorbing my earliest lessons in how not to behave as an adult. We all were constantly playing a funny game in the yard using old ping-pong paddles, Wiffle balls, and tattered badminton nets held together mostly with tape and good wishes. Fond memories of those trips are peppered with visions of Father John and me laughing together in the side yard of my aunt's waterfront home with a backdrop of the Straights of Juan de Fuca and Mount Rainier. Myriad islands and hidden waterways were all as close and vivid as the imagination. I continued this seasonal sojourn for seven summers, the last five of which I remember with striking detail. They constitute my sharpest memories of early times with my father.

In the late 1950s and early 60s, expressions like Pickle-Pong, Pickleball, or sometimes simply "Pickle" were thrown around at the Bechtells' as loosely as that old Badminton net was hung. My first real clue into the double and triple entendre of Pickle came unexpectedly from my mother when, upon my return home from these excursions, she would often ask, "… Were they all pickled?"

The subtleties of Pickle took years for me to fully comprehend. Even now, it is not clear which was the Bechtells' true pickle touchstone. It may have been the various levels of individual and collective inebriation they achieved, or the seemingly never ending supply of homemade Sweet Gherkins, a specialty of my Aunt Gretchen, spawned no doubt from the DNA of her Barbaricum lineage. Sweet Gherkin memory: a satiating and sweet indulgence that I worked diligently to consume in quantities disproportionate to my age and stature.

When my trips to Whidbey Island with Father John finally ceased in 1966, my thoughts about Pickle-Pong, Pickleball, and Pickle in general faded silently into the thickening fog of conflated childhood lore.

As I grew, I became very active in music and the martial arts, creating a composite career from both, gradually supplanting my formative experiences with more mature content until at last, a deeply buried synapse was the only remaining connection I had to anything Pickle.

A score of years and then some passed before I arrived with my own small family in tow for our first summertime respite in, on, and around Lake Sebago in the "Vacationland" of South Central Maine. Frye Island was and is the summer lake home of my wife's lifelong best friend Stephanie, her husband Lew, and their two sons. Frye served for many years as our annual summer retreat from Connecticut. After our first decade of sunny summer days in Maine, over breakfast one morning, Lew and Steph told us of a new game recently introduced to the island, called Pickleball - a fantastic game that they were playing with growing dedication and commitment, rivaling their lengthy love affair with tennis. Tales of this fantastic "new" pastime that evidently all ages could enjoy together rekindled the glowing embers of my quiescent youthful memories into a fresh blaze of recollection.

Investigation, participation, and close observation of this "new" sporting phenom on Frye brought about a creeping familiarity and an awakening realization that I indeed had been witness to and part of the birth of this game. Father John, Gretchen, Chuck, Uncle Chesty, Erminie, Joel, Bill, and their collective related tribes and I had played this game, a game that with some minor tweaks, had become Pickleball.

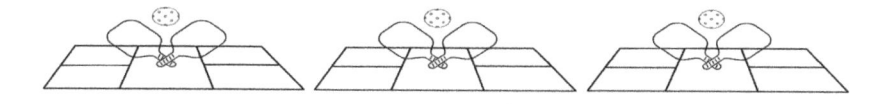

*The Olympic Mountains, west of Seattle,
on the ferry ride from Mukilteo to Whidbey*

*The Pacific Coast, west of the Olympic Mountains,
capturing the Northwest Vibe*

Two

1963

Charles "Chuck" Bechtell was never far from money. That, and his college days on the Gridiron were his touchstones. The pigskin taught him well to plan ahead, yet stay flexible and to be aggressive, but agreeable. Whether it was his own money or someone else's, he was always flush with cash from his many business dealings. He enjoyed spreading it around, too, often as a donor of time, space, and as he would say, "cash money", to the politically liberal and progressive wing of Washington's local and state government, in those days the Republicans, ahh ... how times change.

On a regular basis, Uncle Chuck and my Aunt Gretchen impressively entertained our governing movers and shakers at their quaint and idyllic summer abode. I clearly recall encountering Mr. Joel Pritchard, then of Washington State's House of Representatives, at the Whidbey house during more than one of my family's summertime soirees. Other names from Pickleball lore that spark recollections of passing, if not quite clear, youthful acquaintance were future senator Slade Gorton and Governor Dan Evans, both of whom I recall very clearly. A Mr. McCallum rings a bell, as does Bill Bell, both recognized names in today's references to Pickleball's creation.

My grandmother, Ruth Hubbard, yes ... Old Mother Hubbard, owned at one point thirteen houses that peppered the cardinal and ordinal points of Seattle's compass from Magnolia Bluff to Queen Anne Hill, Capitol Hill across Elliott Bay to West Seattle, and all the way to Alki Point. Images of other similar political events, held at one or more of those locations, flow across the screen of my memories as I reflect upon the summers' activities of those early years. I learned at my family's feet that there was always a hand to be shaken or palm to be greased at a Bechtell gathering, somewhere.

While I do have an unusually good memory and sincerely believe my recollections to be accurate - that all of those early Pickleballers were somehow in that picture - I'd be lying to say I met them all for sure. The memories feel right, but I was after all, only seven years old at the time.

As for '63, I remember the year unquestioningly because during that August vacation on Whidbey Island, my father John presented me with an early 7th birthday gift, the only gift I clearly recall from my entire childhood. It was an awesome red Schwinn two-wheeler tricked out with handlebar streamers, 16-inch wheels, and a speedometer that went up to 50 mph! Father John and I would not be together on my actual seventh birthday, September 7th, hence the early gift. The 7th of September came and went without incident.

Soon, however, that Schwinn, through no fault of its own, would land me along with my poor choices, in a windowless ICU-style room for a seven-day hiatus in the Seattle hospital of my birth, Virginia Mason.

It was a transcendent experience preparing for my hospital visit, rocketing downhill with my speedometer needle pinned, riding "no hands"... glorious, until my tires found the loose gravel at the bottom of the hill, instantly snatching my newly found freedom out from under me. The tarmac came up fast to meet my outstretched arms and dismayed visage. To this day I can instantly conjure a disturbingly graphic image of myself, bleeding from numerous ports with compound right arm fractures, radius and ulna all ways akimbo, suddenly on full display for up-close inspection. A would-be, could-be, and probably should-be poster child for bike helmet safety, I limped home with abrasions to my right eye and gravel imbedded in my face, hands, and legs, leaving the Schwinn in the ditch, like so much roadkill. My shocked mother, who was uncommonly home at the time, silently but surely blamed Father John for my state of ill-repair as she rushed me to the hospital in "Betsy", her maroon '56 Plymouth that ran smoothly and quickly across the old floating bridge to the mainland on fully leaded 28-cent-per-gallon regular gas ... but I digress.

... so much roadkill

Three

A Gherkin Near Rose Point, By Any Other Name, Would Taste As Sweet

For the sake of clarity, to be "pickled" was a slang term used by many during those years to describe a person as being tipsy, three sheets to the wind - my personal favorite, into their cups, or ... just plain drunk.

Among my relatives, being "Pickled" was not an uncommon happenstance. Enter stage left Sweet Gherkins, another **Smith/Bechtell** family favorite. For the uninitiated, Sweet Gherkins are a tart and tantalizing snappy snack that can still be tasted by the dulled senses of those who enjoy to excess the nectar of fermented potato while hacking through cartons of darts from Philip Morris's finest.

The Gherkin, Germanesque for pickle, was ubiquitous at the time of the beginning of Pickleball. It was instrumental in the naming of the Whidbey Island game, as well as the feeding of its earliest (and youngest) players. My aunt "pickled" the Gherkins herself from a very old family recipe, while the libations were provided by Dimple, Smirnoff, and The Rainier Brewing Company. Consumption to the point of "pickling" was, of course, left up to individual choice.

Pickled Pickles in Ball Jars aka Gherkins a la Gretchen

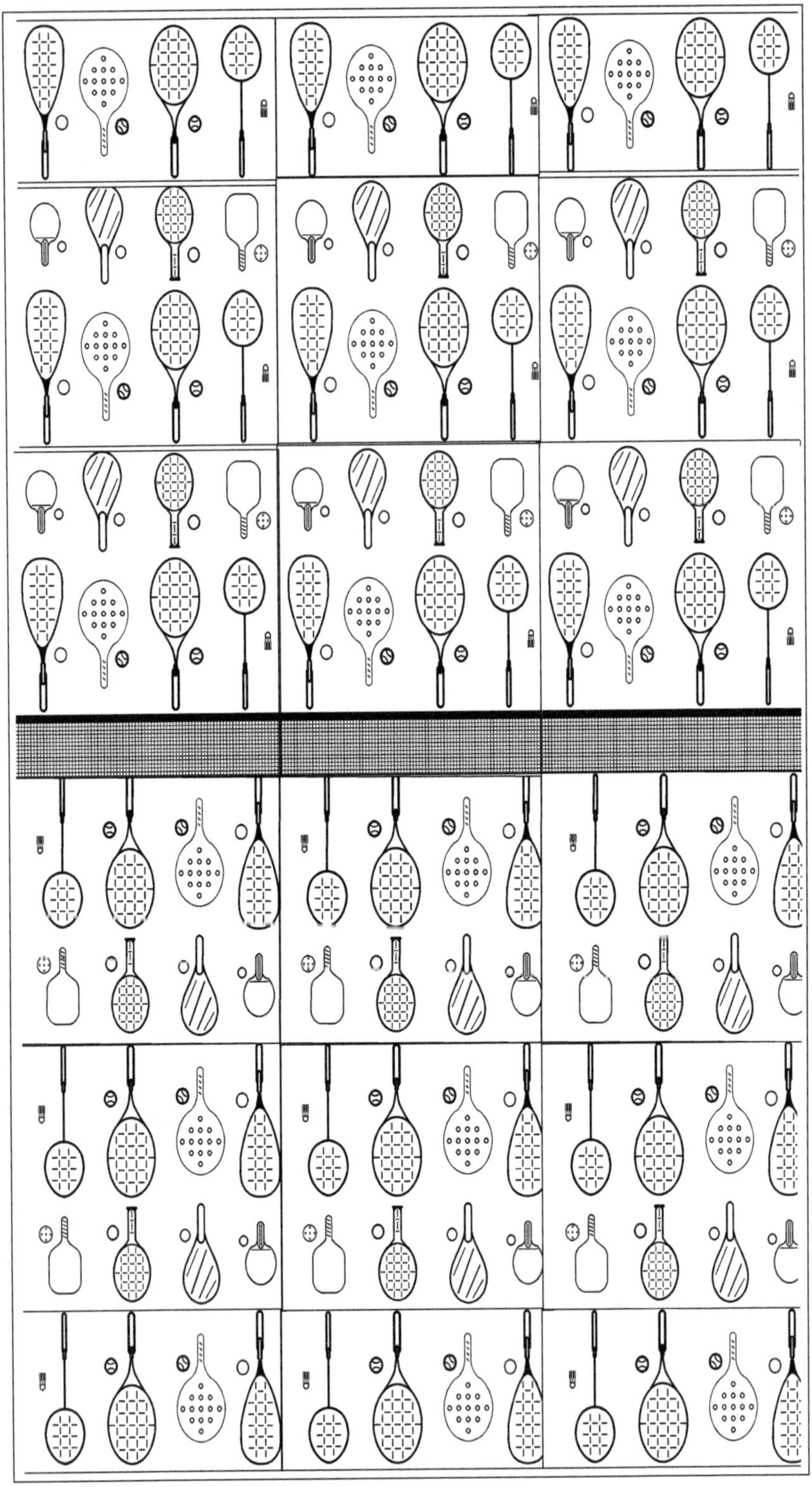

Four

The Lay of the Land • JFK, The Space Needle, Elvis and ...

1962 saw the second year of John F. Kennedy's first and last term as President. The Seattle World's Fair - Century 21 Exposition - opened with the marvel of the Space Needle and the spectacle of Elvis filming on location "It Happened at the World's Fair". Aside from all that, 1962 was important because it was the year that the game now called Pickleball truly came to life. Of course, in 1962, unlike Elvis, Pickleball was unknown. It was a game without a name. Also, unlike Elvis, I was only six.

We all know how it turned out for JFK. As for the Space Needle - now in its seventh decade - it's still standing. It is still what makes the Seattle skyline, THE SEATTLE SKYLINE. As for Elvis's movie, I mention it only because it was Elvis, and I was forced to see a short clip from it many times, in my late teens, by a friend who actually was in it.

I'd love to mention that the Beatles were there in '62 as well, but they didn't come to Seattle until 1964 on their first world tour, a full year before Pickleball would be launched on Bainbridge Island by Mr. Pritchard and friends.

The Fab Four - Fishing at the Edgewater Inn, the only hotel in town that would take them in. *

They stayed at the Edgewater Inn with a nice view of Bainbridge out their fishing window. Their backs were to Elliott Bay while they faced thousands of screaming fans who were held at bay in front of the hotel by a single lonely cordon of cyclone fencing, hastily erected

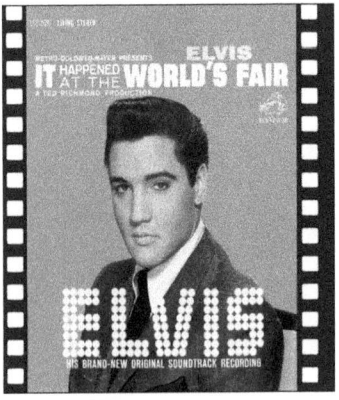

The King

before their arrival. I saw them, too, outside the Edgewater at my mother's side on the occasion of her 48th birthday.

There were, and are, no Pickleball courts at the Edgewater, but now a Day Pass can get you on a court at a sports club two blocks from the hotel. Elvis's film, released in April of 1963, grossed a little over two million 1960's dollars, which by today's inflationary valuation would have been about eight million, small beer for Elvis. And of course, The Beatles became "Paul McCartney's band BEFORE *Wings*".

Alaskan Way, the home to all of these fascinating tidbits, places, and much more definitely deserves a visit if you ever find yourself in the neighborhood.

The Edgewater Inn and The Space Needle, within shouting distance

*If you know your Rock & Roll dark lore, The Edgewater, with its questionable amenity of "...go fishing from your hotel window", played an unwitting yet ignominious role with another band, Led Zeppelin, when in 1969 during their stay at the Edgewater, a sordid incident allegedly took place involving a mudshark that was fished out of Puget Sound from their hotel window - at least according to Frank Zappa. Whether true or false, Seattle continues to this day to be the epicenter of dark and twisted Rock & Roll trivia.

14

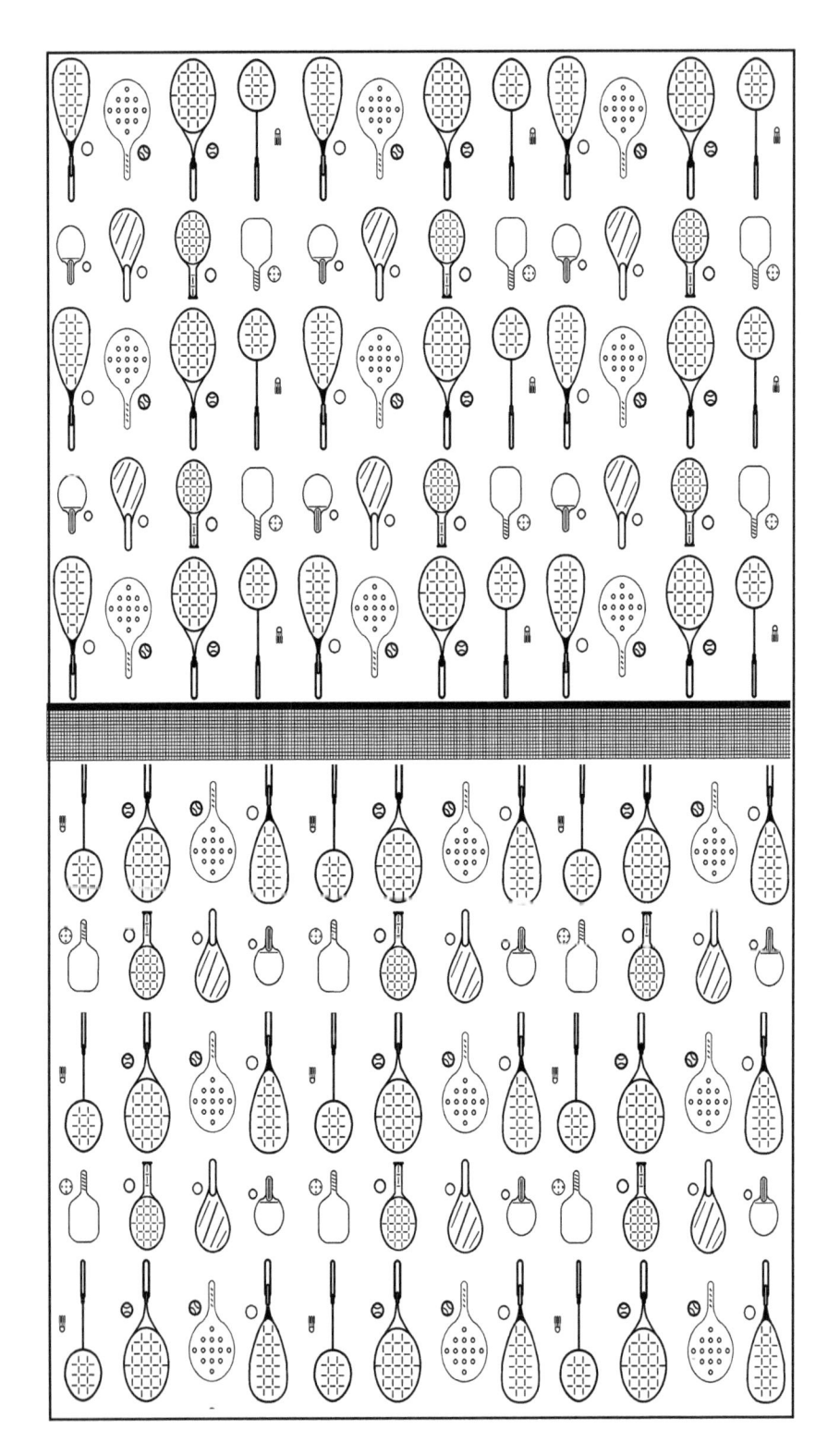

Five

North by Northwest
Pickleball at Ground Zero

Whidbey Island sits about twenty-five nautical miles north of Pickleball's ersatz birthplace - Bainbridge Island - and about twenty fast miles northeast, as the missile flies, of the Trident Nuclear Submarine Base in Bangor, Washington. If you know anything about Connecticut, you might have heard of Electric Boat and the Trident Base at Groton where the Navy's nuclear submarines actually are built. Bangor is Groton's nuclear "sister city" in Washington state, defensively blanketing the northern hemisphere and the Pacific Ring of Fire, ironically named for the volcanic activity that circles the Pacific Ocean, not the nukes in the silos that dot the Pacific Northwest's government-owned habitats.

The side yard of Aunt Gretchen's house on Whidbey

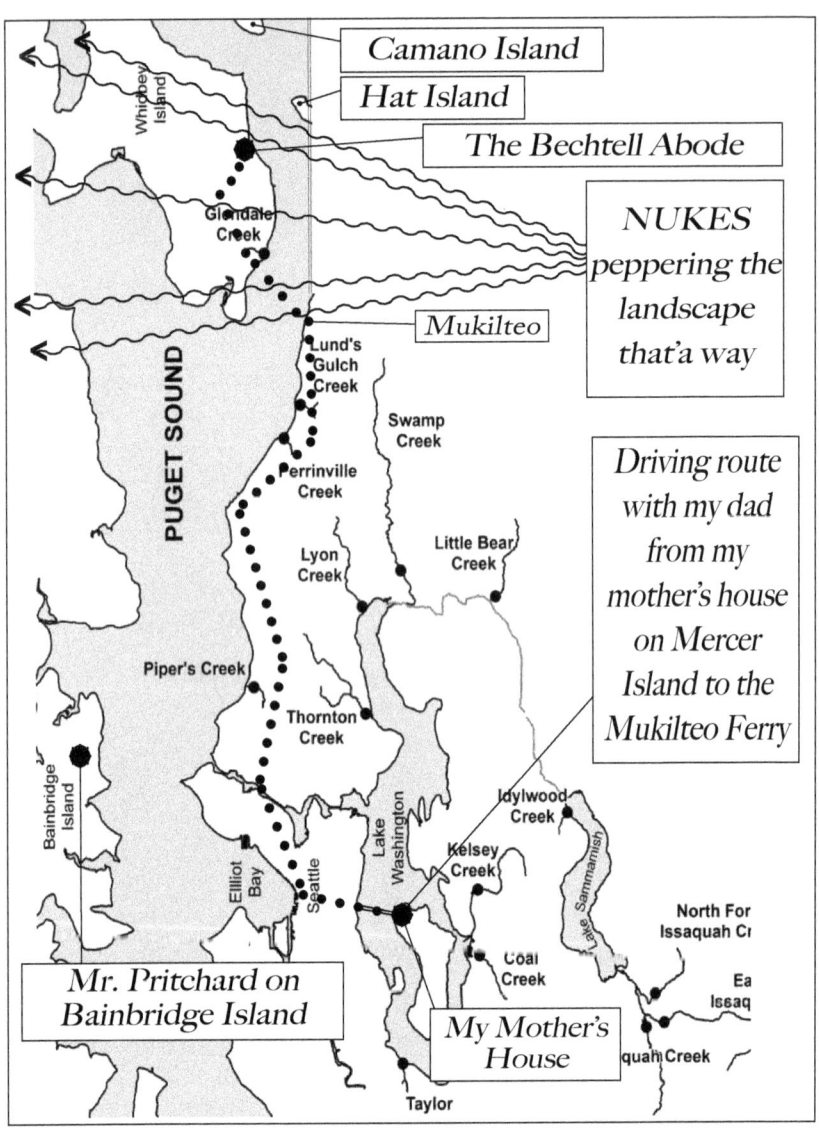

Map labels:
- Camano Island
- Hat Island
- The Bechtell Abode
- NUKES peppering the landscape that'a way
- Mukilteo
- Driving route with my dad from my mother's house on Mercer Island to the Mukilteo Ferry
- Mr. Pritchard on Bainbridge Island
- My Mother's House

Island in northern central Puget Sound would be easy to overlook, were it not for the location. The house itself stood on Whidbey's southeastern water's edge, smack dab between the fishing village of Clinton, the Mukilteo ferry landing, and the larger burg of Langley to the north. The rear bay windows opened directly onto an uninterrupted view of Hat Island, 1000 yards or so due east and the southern tip of Camano Island to the north, just behind her award-winning

16

rose bushes. All of this sat due south of the rest of the San Juan archipelago, Vancouver Island, and the panhandle of Seward's Folly.

In 2010, after two decades of work by Bert Webber, a scientist from my alma mater in nearby Bellingham, the name "The Salish Sea" was established for this region of the Pacific Ocean's northwest waterways, honoring the indigenous Salish-speaking tribes who lived along the coastline of the entire area for more than 6,000 years. Salish is the root language of many of the indigenous dialects found in this region. The Salish Sea extends from southern British Columbia and Vancouver Island in Canada, south to the southern end of Puget Sound at Washington's state capital, Olympia. On any clear day Mount Rainier could be seen in the distance rising above the clouds on the right to the southeast, and Mount Baker if one stood on tippy-toes, with neck craned to the north. All manner of ships, freighters, ferries, the occasional battleship, aircraft carrier, or nuclear submarine, and countless sailboats, orcas, seals, sea lions, and small watercraft would, as a daily occurrence, quietly glide past Gretchen's roses and heavily festooned clotheslines.

The military had and still has a big, albeit quiet, footprint in the area. The Bechtell summer abode was nested within striking distance of the Bremerton Naval Shipyard, where many of our WWII aircraft carriers have been mothballed after decommissioning. Continuing northeast for twenty more miles, the city of Everett was the home of the Boeing Aircraft plant, where if necessary, THREE 747s could be built entirely from the ground up in any given 24-hour cycle.

Given its geographic coordinates, my aunt's Whidbey Island home, the epicenter of Pickleball creation in 1962,

The Missiles of October

Likely Target Selections During the Cuban Missile Crisis of October 1962

easily could have become absolute Ground Zero on October 22nd if Premier Khrushchev had had anything more to say about it. John F. Kennedy dodged that bullet, but exactly thirteen months later, November 22, 1963, the next bullet got him. Along with my mother, I cried. Very Sad …

Six

Local Color ~ Then and Now

Harper's Weekly Magazine • August 22, 1891 • pg. 691 • Detail of The Gold Regions Explored by General Custer showing the Indian Reservations and Military Posts in the Western United States. Massive expansion into the West, only 20 years after Chief Seattle's letter was drafted. (see Appendix 1)

My father, John Smith ... yes, really, was something of a black sheep in the Smith/Bechtell family tree. He married outside the faith - Steerike ONE; he got divorced eighteen months later - Steeerike TWO; and in the process, got himself what his family thought of as a Bastard Son ... ME - STEEEERIKE THREE! You are OUTTA'Theyaa'. Also, factor in that he didn't get into medical school to follow in HIS father's footsteps ... regardless, in spite of it all, he dotingly ferried me from Mercer Island in King County to Mukilteo in Snohomish County for a visit at his sister's summer home on Whidbey, North of Bainbridge in Island County, repeating this exercise continuously for several years, on most weekends throughout the spring, summer, and fall months. For him, Whidbey was his weekend getaway from a steady but dull job at Boeing in Everett. Our weekends were the relaxing Yang to his work-a-day Yin.

Mukilteo was a quaint village and the former stomping ground of the Lushootseed-Mukilteo Snohomish Indians who had lived there for several thousands of years, ending abruptly in about 1855. Likely under duress, they signed it all over to English explorer George Vancouver in the Treaty of Point Elliot. The location would eventually be renamed Rose Point for the predominance of the thorny flower that smelled as sweet. Soon, white settlers from "back east" would arrive in droves and pine tree logging would begin in earnest, only to be followed forty-three years later by an even bigger disaster, the Alaskan Gold Rush. So much for the sovereign Snohomish Nation.

After the Point Elliot treaty went into effect, the Tulalip, Salish, Snohomish, Skagit, Nisqually, Duwamish, Suquamish, Snoqualmie, Lummi, and other local tribes maintained encampments along the coastline of Puget Sound, preserving at least some of their traditional hunting and fishing grounds until late in the 19th century.

Twenty-five miles to the south of Mukilteo is the city bearing the name of the Chief of the Suquamish and Duwamish, Chief Seattle. Now, as the home of the Boeing "Future of Flight Museum", today's fully gentrified Mukilteo boasts one of the higher income brackets in all of Washington State.

Of the nine islands that comprise Island County, Whidbey Island is the largest. The town of Coupeville is the county seat, about twenty-five miles north/northwest of my aunt's place. Once surrounded by fishing villages, that section of Whidbey is now, *unofficially*, surrounded by an *undisclosed* number of what *might* be first-strike nuclear missiles that *could* be, but *probably aren't*, nested in somewhat hidden missile silos, that *might* pepper that part of the Puget Sound geography, particularly on Whidbey Island. Of course I have never really seen them with my own eyes, *except for all of the times I did* ... unofficially speaking.

In 1854, Chief Seattle gave a speech (Appendix 1), prompted by a meeting that was called by then-Governor Issac I. Grant, the "White Chief", to discuss the disposition of Native lands through surrender or sale to the arriving white settlers from the East. The first English translation of Chief Seattle's speech was offered up by Dr. Henry A. Smith through at least two third-party translations, the first from the original Lushootseed dialect into Chinook, and then into English by Dr. Smith. The good Doctor then published his version in a local Seattle paper of the day, the *Seattle Sunday Star*.

With caveats it is reported that Chief Seattle expressed, among other things, his concern over the treatment of the land and people by the new white settlers. He warned against abusing the environment but accepted the arrival of the white people from the East. He predicted that the Native tribal days were numbered and counseled his people to accept their future peacefully to avoid complete extinction at the hands of the new settlers, or words to that effect. Authentic or apocryphal, it is a powerful message worthy of another look. See Appendix 1, if you would like to read Dr. Smith's translation. While I myself come from a long line of doctors, I'm not sure if Dr. Henry A.

> Smith is my great, great, great, ... great grandfather or not, and anyone in my clan who might have known for sure has long since gone to spirit. Alas, another link, the veracity of which is also lost in the fog of history.

Chief Si'ahl (Seattle)
circa 1750-60 to 1866

Taken in 1864, this is the only known photograph of Chief Si'ahl.

Courtesy of The Museum of History & Industry - SHS67 - Seattle, Washington

Seven

Itinerary Ad Libitum ~ The Same Old, Same Old

Photo Credit - Museum of History & Industry, Seattle, WA

Washington State Ferry KALAKALA - "The Silver Swan" July 5, 1935 in Elliott Bay, soon to pass The Smith Tower, which was for 50 years the tallest building west of the Rocky Mountains.

My usual agenda when visiting Aunt Gretchen on Whidbey included the long car ride from my house on Mercer Island, westward across the mile long (old) "floating bridge" crossing Lake Washington. We then continued through downtown Seattle and shot north on the Alaskan Way Viaduct, which ran parallel to Elliott Bay. By then Father John's old aquamarine Renault would need a rest. The car would recuperate during a brief stop at the Hiram M. Chittenden "Government Locks" where we watched the boats and small ships ride up and down the twenty-

23

Sporting a "Century 21" advertising panel for the 1962 World's Fair, KALAKALA sails west, soon to pass Alki Point on her port side in West Seattle, making her midday sojourn to Bremerton.

two feet of differential in elevation between the salt water of Puget Sound and the fresh waters of Green Lake and Lake Washington, the "Sailing Capitol of the World". In 1962, there were more sailboats than cars in Seattle.

After witnessing the engineering spectacle of The Locks and feeding breadcrumbs – "quackers" to ubiquitous ducks, the Ballard Mallards, we would drive further north through "Swedetown", aka Ballard, on up the back roads to Mukilteo and its tiny Washington State ferryboat landing.

Then and now, Puget Sound boasts the most active and coordinated ferry fleet anywhere in the world. My favorite boat of the fleet was the *Kalakala*, which evidently means bird in the language of the Chinook Indians, another tribe from the greater Seattle area. She was a very space age-looking

Super-Ferry WENATCHEE coming in to Colman Dock, Pier 52, likely on a return trip from Bremerton or Bainbridge Island.

craft, befitting the times, with a shiny burnished silver aircraft-style aerodynamic profile that never really managed to run right. Even with the Chadburn engine controls at only Half Ahead, she vibrated disturbingly while underway. The *Kalakala* looked, to many people including my father, like a giant floating suppository. The Ballard Scandinavians called her the Kackerlacka, the floating Cockroach. Though she was sleek and sexy in a 1960's futuristic sort of way, she never fit in with the classic open designs of all of the other ferries in the fleet.

Sadly, she was ultimately sold and towed to Alaska, where she was ignominiously converted into a crab cannery. Fifty-two years after my introduction to her, she was returned to Puget Sound and her final resting place at the docks in Tacoma, south of Seattle. The *Kalakala*'s last rites were at last read when, in 2015 under a cloud of contention and environmental concern, the *Kalakala*'s decaying shell was repurposed in sections for metal scrap reclamation and artistic sculptural usage. In the end, flotsam and jetsam shoreside was all her storied life had remaining. Rest In Peace, old girl.

Sean Griffin - Photographer • photo gratefully used with permission

Here in the Hylebos Waterway in Tacoma, KALAKALA found her final resting place where she languished for a decade before being sold for scrap.

After the short westerly transit of the comparatively diminutive Mukilteo ferry, Father John and I would disembark in Clinton, a mile or so south of Gretchen's. After landing, we would then go forthwith to my aunt's property, where settling in, saying hello to everyone, and relaxing for a drink or two *or three* was the standard order of the day. Verboten in my mother's house, I always settled in by adding a little life with a Coke and a smile. That Coke would not become a "classic" for another twenty-two years in early 1985, nor was it the "original" Coke that had the good stuff instead of sugar. Tradition dictated that we would soon make our way down the sloping rear yard, to then descend a steep and rickety set of wooden steps that led to the abruptly chilly water's edge and my father's modest dinghy for a variably buoyant and listing lesson in fishing that never bore fruit, or fish, for that matter.

I believe now that the consistent failures of our fishing ventures were somehow disappointing to my father, but it was just as well since my mother was raising me as a strict vegetarian. So strict in fact, that unbeknownst to us all, the diet I was on had been described as vegan for almost eighteen years already. Our fishing faux pas would be followed by conciliatory ice cream at a local shop. Apparently my father didn't get the memo about veganism and dairy products, either. Ice cream was followed by another ride in the car, past the aforementioned missile silos, to lunch at the waterfront seafood joint in Langley where the only things on the menu I could eat were the green salad and French fries, again because of the vegan thing. We ended the ritual with the subsequent ride back to my Aunt Gretchen's for more settling in. Another Coke for me, the source of all my childhood dental issues.

Mount Rainier - 14,411 feet of Nature's Good Stuff

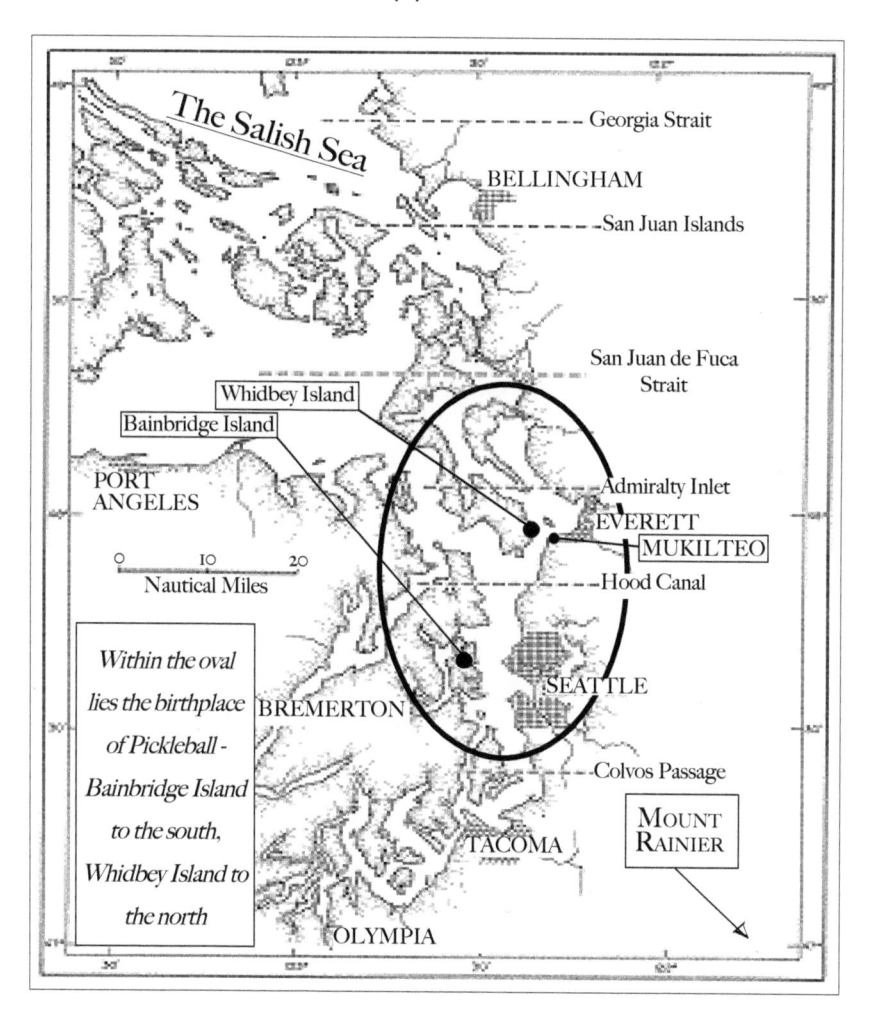

Within the oval lies the birthplace of Pickleball - Bainbridge Island to the south, Whidbey Island to the north

28

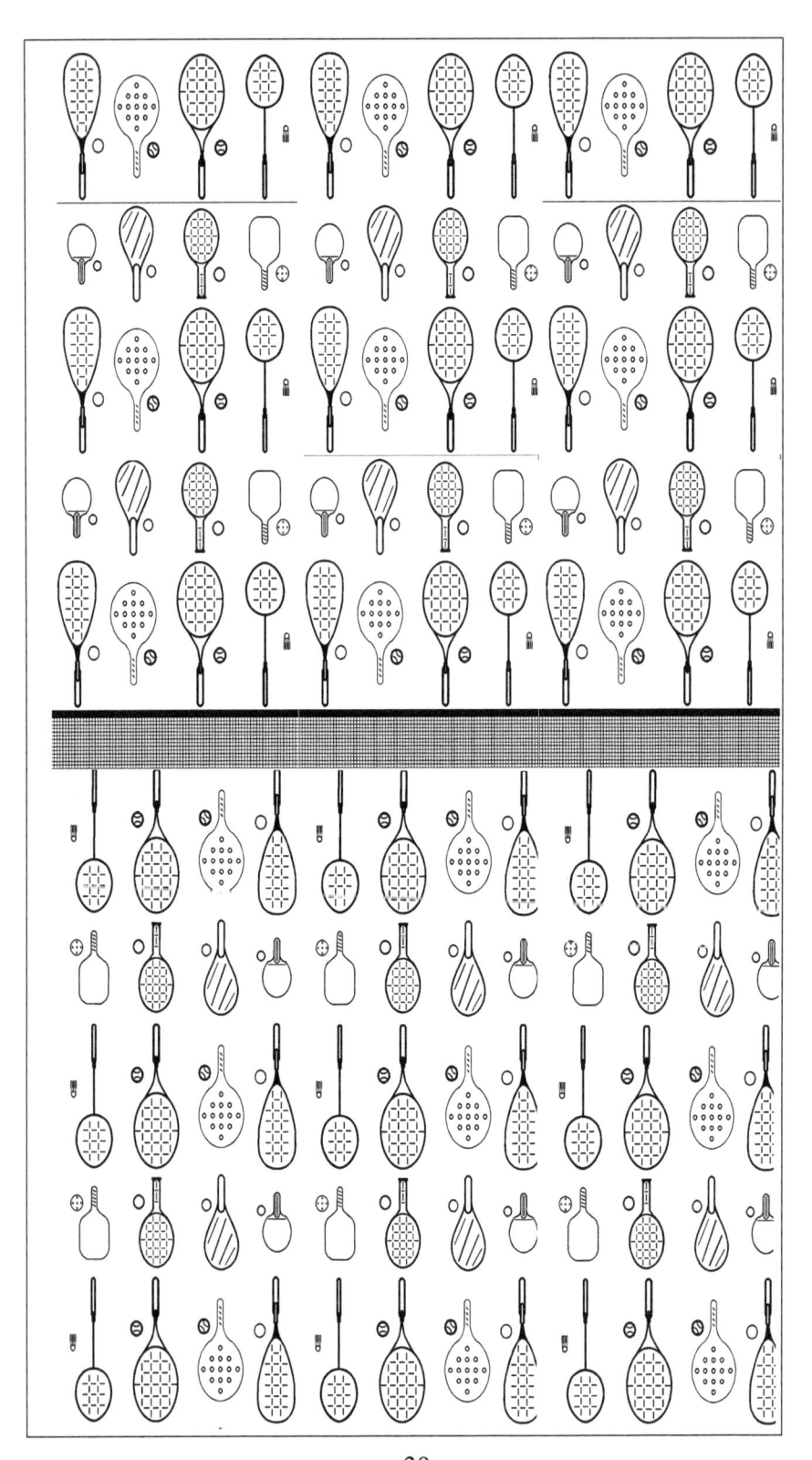

Eight

Preparation of the Pitch

I was first alerted to a change in routine when one day Uncle Chesty pulled an old push lawnmower from the shed and began to mow the side yard that he referred to as the "pitch", a term he borrowed from cricket I suppose. *Sha-ka-ta Sha-ka-ta, Sha-ka-ta - Sha-ka-ta Sha-ka-ta, Sha-ka-ta*, the aged mower tore at the grass, heaving angrily back and forth under Chesty's determined jackhammering ministrations. More ripped than clipped by the dull and rusted tool, the lawn was at last shredded to an acceptable height for whatever outdoor activity was soon to ensue.

After the "Trimming of the Pitch" had ceased and a furtive gesture had been made at rearranging the detritus, Chesty's preparation of the gaming court had reached its questionable apex. Trundling his now shirtless 300-plus pounds, running rivulets of sweat, Chesty went back to the shed wherefrom he extracted a flimsy, rather unstable net-like apparatus. With no small effort, this netting was staked to the ground between the violently invading forsythia that had taken Gretchen's rose garden by force and the newly installed pebbled concrete driveway. Pebbled concrete is a surface that features very small, very smooth and round stones encrusted immovably into its hard surface. When damp, this driveway surfacing material can take on the challenging characteristics of ball bearings. On this day, with no shade in sight, the driveway was very hot and slick with the remaining glazing of grass trimmings that carpeted its nearest edge, a cement sobriety test waiting patiently to dole out a harsh consequence to any unsuspecting inebriate.

    Liberating the required equipment included the unearthing of a disintegrating but authentic G.I. (government issue) duffle bag, which was ejected from the shed next. Several discarded and well used wooden, natural gut-strung sawed off tennis rackets, notably flaccid from ill use, plus a larger number of peeling ping-pong paddles appeared from inside the darkening canvas Navy bag. The bag itself was a remnant of Chesty's days on the high seas of the South Pacific, sporting as it did the Bickford name in fading black ink, all caps. Each racket had the earmarks of long and unfortunate use. They all had roughly cut off handles that were about six inches in length and wrapped with surprising care in high adhesion black electrical tape. "Airplane tape", according to Chesty, which had been co-opted from a shop at the Boeing Everett plant, the same plant where the aforementioned 747s were assembled from parts shipped in from around the country.

Johnny must have boosted this very fancy tape from the jet assembly areas he oversaw at Boeing. I am positive that he had personally done the tape application to the racket and paddle handles. A good pianist in his own right, enhanced by a touch of OCD, Father John had finesse. Boeing housed all of their aerospace stuff, like Teflon tape, at Plant 2 and Boeing Field, just south of Seattle proper. Boeing Field was the home of their concept jet, the Boeing Supersonic Transport – The SST. Chuck held a managerial position there and, unlike Johnny, probably did not spend much time on the shop floor shoplifting. He didn't spend any time on the SST initiative either, mover and shaker that he was. If he had been on that project, the US government might not have pulled funding on the program in 1971, leaving the Franco/Anglo Concorde to cruise alone at 1350 mph, a little over one mile every three seconds, more than eleven miles straight up.

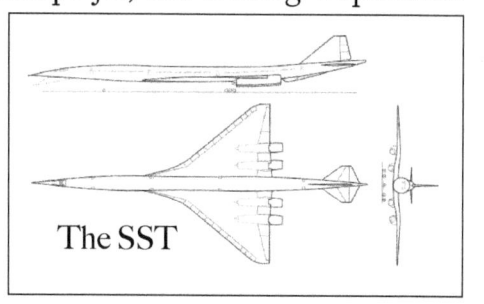

The SST

Next from the duffle's depths, the Wiffle ball emerged. I noticed that with age and abuse it had attained, over the span of its tired career, the grayish off-white pallor with the furry feel of polyethylene balls that have skidded on concrete and caromed off garage doors times beyond number.

With a sidelong questioning glance at me, having completed the installation, Chesty ponderously lurched toward the side door of the house, which led directly into the kitchen. Upon entry he announced in no uncertain terms that he was ready for a drink! "Get out of my kitchen! I Never Serve in The

Kitchen," Gretchen boomed, "and for GOD's *sakes*, put on a shirt!" I can only imagine what was said in muffled tones that I could not follow from my post on the pitch.

Surprise shook me when Chesty finally yelled over Gretchen's squawking, "The pitch is ready!"

Aunt Gretchen's Kitchen, a rendering by the author, or someone like him ...

Nine

The Necessary Accoutrements

The flaccid net of bygone days, ubiquitous in the beginning

In short order there emerged a parade of small tables littered with plates of small foods, bowls of assorted snacks, glasses, goblets, tankards, and snifters of multi-colored foul-smelling concoctions that did nothing but burn my tender snot locker when I got close enough to actually inhale their caustic humors. A separate table, placed off to one side and flanked by chaise loungers, seemed to be designated for occupation by only two items. Most obvious was a large and gleaming chromium ashtray topsy-turvy with a confused muddle of filterless Camels, Chesterfield Kings, and Lucky Strikes for the men and filter tipped Kents and Marlboros for the ladies. I could actually taste their noisome funk from across the yard.

The second item was a garish ceramic dish of questionable origin and unidentifiable color that was littered with small, acrid yet enticing too green pickle-ettes. I asked my father what they were and between drags on his Camel, he said they were Gherkins. I said I thought they were called pickle-ettes. He responded, "No, they are Gretchen's own sweet Gherkins; try one." Offering me access to his drink he said, "Dip your finger, then lick it fast, and pop a Gherkin in your mouth, and chew it up." Recall if you will that I was SIX, being offered a finger dip of Scotch… but I did as he suggested - was repulsed by the Dimple, yet overjoyed by the Gherkin. My father and Chuck got a good laugh at my squinched face as Gretchen loudly proclaimed my father to be an idiot. "You'll get him pickled," she said. "He'll tell his mother, then that will be that." I never shared that story with my mother.

Aunt Gretchen and Uncle Chuck had an astoundingly annoying mongrel whose name was decidedly NOT Pickles. They called him "Lacey", which I came to understand was their affectionate nickname for Laces, so named by Uncle Chuck for the stitching on the side of an early football, his hat tip to the pigskins of Walter Camp's Yale Bulldogs circa 1880-1900. Laces was for Chuck a self-referential reminder of his halcyon days on the gridiron at UDub, the University of Washington, where he evidently played football and, in his spare time, learned how to DO the business that he was now quite successful in doing, between liquid lunches.

Lacey somehow had decided it was a good idea to nip at me when I wasn't looking. He was one of those yapping little beasts. With quaffed mane of dull off-white fur, Lacey more resembled a low riding dark cumulus than he did an actual affection-meriting best friend of man, woman, or anything else. Lacey was an early foray into cross-breeding – some sort of Pomeranian-Chihuahua hybrid. A healthy dose of little doggy narcissism, courtesy of Chuck, was deeply infused into his psyche. Eating food from your plate, humping your leg, mewling incessantly when not the center of attention, and just as likely to defecate in your palm as lick it, Lacey was a product of his environment. Ivan Pavlov himself could not have done a better job of classical conditioning. Lacey learned well at the feet of his master, Chuck Bechtell.

In preparation for a match of Pickle, harkening back I think to his youthful athleticism, Chuck chose a particular sawed-off tennis racket, which he clutched in a stoic death grip. The other players, having only a limited recent association with anything terribly strenuous, elected their preferred yet sorry looking ping-pong paddles.

With the players swatting at invisible bugs to gain the feel of their personal Wiffle-whacking weapons of choice, the stage was set for battle as the Bechtell clan took up stations at pre-ordained positions on the "pitch". My father and I were sidelined, with me as errant ball boy, Father John as the Dimple-nursing net and line judge.

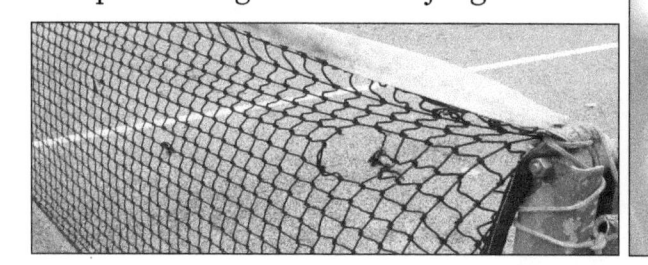

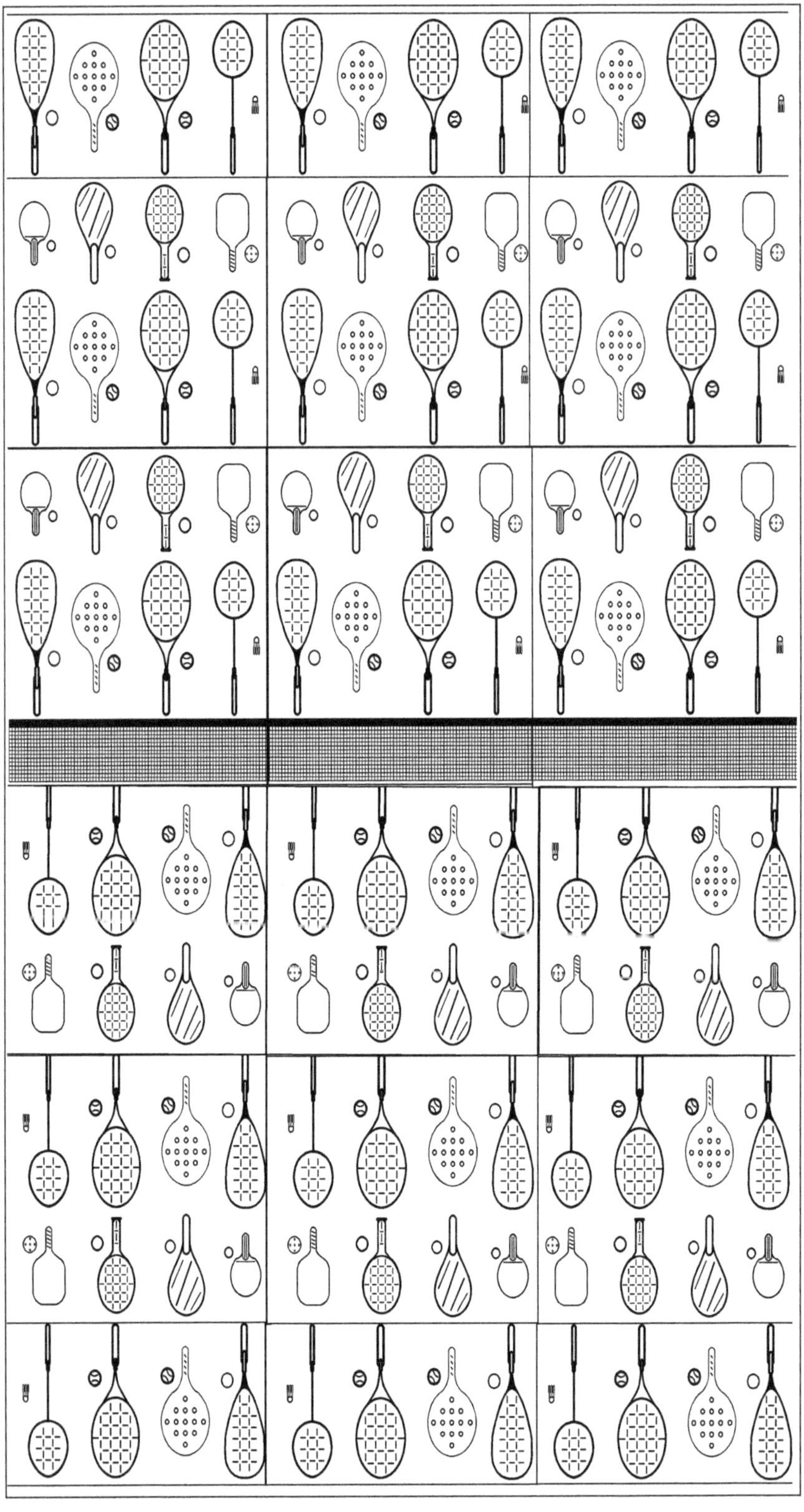

Ten

The Playbill

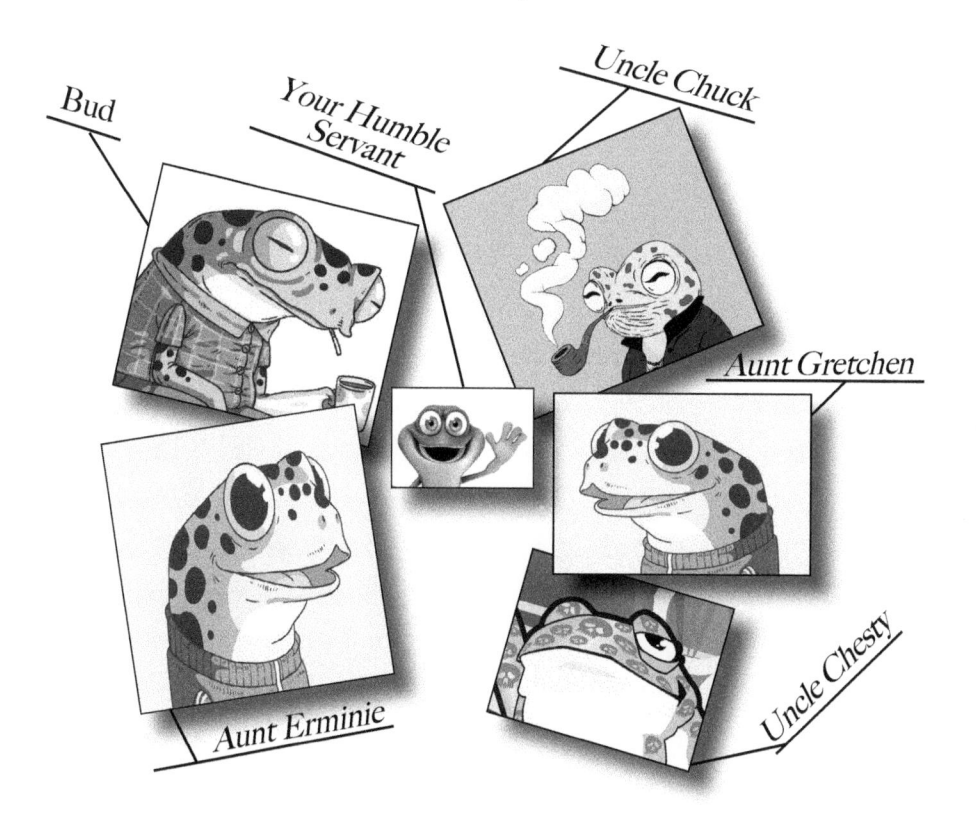

Gretchen Bechtell; her brother and my father John Smith, aka Johnny or *Bud*; their sister Erminie Bickford; Gretchen's husband Uncle Chuck; and Erminie's husband, Uncle Chesty, made up the small but notable brain-trust of Pickleball creation.

Chuck was a businessman - all business, all the time. He had perfected the art of the 1960's Business *Liquid* Lunch, which he enjoyed year-round, on or off work. Chuck was at best boisterous but was more often overbearing, like many businessmen of his generation. Chesty on the other hand was quietly unassuming, living on Naval disability from the Second Big War. On any given day, being well into his cups, Chesty could be seen heeling around from port to starboard, drowning some distant demon. Johnny was a quiet and retiring lifelong Boeing employee, a veteran of the WWII European Theater where he served as a field medic resulting in what I now realize was severe PTSD. He self-medicated this condition with a variety of alternating fermented substances, augmented by Roche Pharmaceutical's new anti-anxiety drug Librium, along with four packs of filterless Camels a day, consumed in the classic chain style, 24/7/365, an extremely expensive habit now that cost only a buck a day back then.

Gretchen and Erminie were gritty and shrill in voice, thanks to the sixty or so Chesterfield darts they both fired up each day. Appealing to feminine society, Virginia Slims were launched in 1968 by Philip Morris Tobacco, shortly after Chesterfield added their "silly millimeter" to the already popular decimeter long smokes. All three brands appealed to my mother. Sixty 101 millimeter cigarettes laid end to end equals almost twenty feet of tobacco to smoke each day, nearly 1.37 miles per year. *I'd walk a mile for a Camel* takes on a new meaning for me now. As the active resident secondhand smoker, by the age of six or seven I had surely tried them all.

Gretchen and Chuck had three daughters who were always "away" somewhere, while Erminie and Chesty were childless, thanks, I believe, to another more particular sort of closeted demon that he was continually struggling to drown in his cups.

Eleven

Let The Games Begin

Chesty had his back to the forsythia and its thorny rose companions, the sun was in his eyes with Gretchen planted on his left, maintaining her preferred proximity to the libations. While Father John was downright svelte compared to Chesty, the aggregate mass of the Bechtell clan had to exceed a metric ton. Together Chesty and Gretchen created an impressive wall of resistance in excess of 500 pounds. Chuck and Erminie, more agile in their presentation, adopted a ready but visibly unstable stance due to the lubricating effects of excess pickling. With the sun advantageously at their backs, they had failed to notice their precarious proximity to the silently waiting grass-slickened pebbled concrete.

Chesty dealt the first ball underhanded with a hidden grace, born of experience. Chuck received and returned with equal skill, and the game was on. To my surprise, they were all smiling and laughing as the ball traversed the space between them in its oddly slow-arching tangent. Traveling far slower than a tennis ball, the two teams had ample time to react and move to positions of advantage on the Pitch. A pleasant and resounding THWOK when the Wiffle was squarely hit with the ping-pong paddle punctuated their every move, the sound sadly absent with Chuck's racket. I had never seen them so happy. Even Father John had a slight upward tilt to his lips. The remarkable grace of their intricate and combined moves, in spite of their meaty frames, bordered on something nearly artistic.

In 1940, Walt Disney released a film that featured hippopotamus ballerinas. Disney's film, "Fantasia", was and is an animated masterpiece featuring Leopold Stokowski and the Philadelphia Orchestra performing many popular classical pieces that serve as a super-sonic palette, colorfully accompanying Walt's visually graphic genius. Chesty's pickled moves were reminiscent of Disney's corpulent ballerinas mincing to Maestro Amilcare Ponchielli's "Dance of the Hours" from his opera "La Gioconda", a tune you might recognize – *"Hello, Mudda…, Hello, Fadda…, here I am at…, Camp Granada…"*, created by a composer you've likely never heard of and music that was misappropriated by 1960s pop culture. My mother was a trained, if not a performing, concert pianist. Strains of Ponchielli's music, a favorite of hers to practice on Sunday afternoons, echoed in my head as I watched the Bechtell quartet shuffle, sashay, mince, and glide as gracefully as Disney's imagination, around the pickle-pitch.

The Bechtell clan clearly had been working at this for some time before my addition to their cast. Focused intently on the scene before us, my father sat next to me, the tumbler of what I now understood to be Dimple Scotch in his left hand and a Camel in his right. With nearly two inches of ash balanced on the smoking embers, forgotten and dangling from his browning nicotined fingers, his right wrist lay limp on the arm of the chaise lounge. In his attention to play, he had not taken a drag for over half a smoke.

Heated volleys of some duration ensued with points taken and given, each one punctuated by laughter and friendly chiding. Bouncing was not a choice with the grass Pitch in this, the first iteration of the game, so a brisk attack on each play was the order of the day. The Bounce, I am sure, was introduced sometime later by the Pritchards of Bainbridge, when the germ of the game was transplanted from my aunt's grassy knoll of a sideyard to their tennis court.

The play had reached a "fever on the pitch" when I noticed that Erminie seemed to be experiencing a noticeably unstable axial list, staring distantly at something that no one but she could see. Clearly, Aunt Erm had lost track of her tenuous position on the edge of The Pitch and her perilous proximity to the grass-slickened pebbly pavement when suddenly and without warning, time slowed.

Seeing that Erminie was not going to intercept an incoming volley that was headed to her outside, Chuck sloshed to his left to pick up the furry, whistling orb before it landed and in so doing, clipped Erminie on her right ankle. He got the ball before it hit the ground with a winding lofty southpaw uppercut that took it completely off The Pitch, sending him in a remarkably elegant diving left shoulder roll, not unlike "The Green Hornet's" Kato, played by the great Bruce Lee. A completed roll had Chuck back on his feet, trumpeting a cry of self satisfaction and glee ... ahhh, the gridiron. The Wiffle ball, having gone unnoticed by all but me, had sailed in its own smoothly parabolic and softly singing arc, through the open screenless kitchen window, sending a tintinnabulation of breaking glass back outside to announce for anyone who heard, the location of the Wiffle's final resting place in the kitchen.

Chuck's save, his dive-roll, and the crash together had taken all of five seconds. Erminie, having been unbalanced by a man three times her size, was left teetering backward with only her left foot to save her rapidly deteriorating verticality. A shuffle step onto the greasy, grassy leftovers of Chesty's Pitch prep was all that was required to set in irreversible motion her now impending and unavoidable structural failure. In their best ball-bearing style, the embedded pebble stones of the new driveway, lubricated as they were by the soggy remnants of Chesty's yard work, sent Erminie tuchus over teakettle in a tangential descent to what ended as a crackling rump slap of an "umph" as she hit the deck with a full-on fanny flop. Cellulite never sounded so good. Father John guffawed before he could contain his surprise. Chuck, partially deaf, gazing quizzically toward the kitchen windows, and still enjoying his triumphant yet pointless save, missed it all.

Now Gretchen, as though pushed by the combined yet invisible force of Erminie's landing, Chuck's dive roll, the crash emitting from her precious kitchen, and of course with no help beyond the Smirnoff, found herself maladroitly cascading backward into her own beloved roses - roses that happily greeted her rotund nether regions, offering a generous and welcoming thorny cushion. Her cries of shock, disbelief, and outrage were, I am sure, raising some eyebrows on Hat Island, half a mile across the eastern waters. Johnny, not having moved from his net/line judge position, now pulled a hefty drag on his previously forgotten dart, at last spilling the lengthy tendril of stubborn ash onto his sharply creased pant leg. Brushing it off as quickly as was his way with any annoyance, I heard Father murmur quietly and to no one in particular, "Who's pickled now, Gretch?" … Schadenfreude!

Recoiling a little as he watched his wife Gretchen splash down into her rosy throne, Chuck turned away to assist with Erminie's recovery. At that moment I decided I would go retrieve the ball, the ball in which everyone but me seemed to have lost interest.

In her shocked and inebriated state, Erminie was assisted to my ball boy lawn chair by Uncle Chuck, where it was determined that she was in fact unharmed. Only then did the official search begin for the missing Wiffle, which I had by then already retrieved.

My father was in a moderate state of tipsy disbelief over this turn of events, and Chesty, Gretchen, and Chuck were all yelling, accusing one another of being the most "pickled". Sighting the unfortunate foot-fault foul perpetrated upon Erminie by the clearly "Pickled" Chuck, everyone forgot once again that they were looking for the ball. The dark humor of the situation was, apparently, lost upon all participants but one.

With the cacophony left behind, I had found the ball not just in the kitchen, but dead center in the sink drain, where it had upset a tray that had toppled what was now an assortment of broken flutes, snifters, and goblets. Chuck may have lost the point, but he had made a hole-in-one. Upon my return to the yard, sporting the Wiffle in hand, Chuck asked me where I had found the ball. "In the kitchen sink," I replied, "some glasses got broken."

Chuck patted me on the back, took the ball, and grabbed a fist full of Gherkins saying, as he aggressively thrust them into my hands, "Here, eat these, Bud," using his nickname for my father.

Chesty and Father John were tending to Erminie. Gretchen was visibly upset as she gingerly extracted thorns from her more personal geography. My uncle and I stood together, taking in the scene. "In the Kitchen sink," Chuck mused, mostly to himself …, "Nice dink, don't you think? Too bad Joel wasn't here to see it."

Dismissing Erminie to the care of her husband, visibly nonplussed by this recent turn of events, Father John returned to his assigned chaise lounge. Settling in for the second time that day, he laid spark to a fresh dart and reflectively sipped at his highball tumbler of Dimple, keeping his own council in the waning incandescence of late afternoon.

I left Whidbey the next day, seldom to return. My mother and I moved far to the south in Washington State, forcing paternal visitations to be significantly curtailed due to excessive distance. Pickleball had been born, but its nurturing was yet to begin.

Twelve
~ WHERE WE ARE NOW ~

Pickleball Now ~ It's Just Competitive Enough

Tennis Courts converted to Pickleball Courts on Frye Island

It is just competitive enough; when I see a foursome that spans as many generations fighting it out, with everyone breaking a little sweat but able to compete, I know I'm seeing something special and amazing. The foursome of which I speak was sporting a sixty-year age bracket between them. Granddad was in his early 70s, Grandma in her mid 60s, Mom was in her early 40s, and the young son/grandson was 15. Mom, playing with her son and her parents in an actual physical game, was visibly moved, with a bright smile she could not have hidden if she tried. She loved being able to play with her son AND her own parents in the same game.

The grandson was genuinely challenged by the level of play and simultaneously supported by the grandfather who was playing hard and keeping his grandson on his toes. Grandma was able to root for the grandson and still score points on him. It was an excellent and beautiful demonstration of the importance of intergenerational connection, love, and tradition-sharing, without the interference of any media or technology beyond what was with them on the court. Sincere competition, connection, and compassion were all the natural result of this gaming interaction. This sight is a daily occurrence on Frye during the summer months and a growing experience worldwide.

On Frye Island in central Maine, for two hours every Monday, Wednesday, Friday, and Sunday, the side-by-side double tennis courts have been converted into Pickleball courts, utilizing the permanent tennis nets as a backboard or *Gherkin Line (my term)* for each Pickle court. Twenty four players at a time dance around this pickle quad, switching in and out, yelling, laughing, smiling, enjoying each other and the fun of the game. Pickleball is "just competitive enough."

As I learned as a child in the early matches at my aunt's house, laughter, joy, and general happiness are a significant part of Pickleballing. Unlike other competitive games, Pickleball is without a doubt one of the most physically sustainable and emotionally healthy sports around.

Thirteen

Our Sensational Conflation Nation ~ Chickens, Eggs, who cares which came first?!

A little mathematical order of operations...
1. Karl Benz ✝ Eli Whitney ⇌ Henry Ford
2. Nicola Tesla ✝ Elon Musk ⇌ TESLA Vehicles
3. The Families Smith/Bechtell ✝ The Families Pritchard/Bell/McCallum ⇌ *Pickleball*

Karl Benz first invented the car in Germany in 1885 or so. At the time, Henry Ford of Greenfield Township, Michigan was about twenty-three years old. Later, in 1901 at age 39ish, Mr. Ford built an assembly line and developed the first affordable automobile (in North America). He is often noted as having "invented" the car, not just the modern assembly line. Ford famously paid his employees $5 a day so they could enjoy a "good living wage" and eventually "buy one of my cars!"

Henry Ford did not invent the car. He merely made it popular and within reach for many people, due largely to his assembly lines. Truth be told, Henry Ford owes more than a hat tip to one of the true creators of the assembly line in the United States - Mr. Eli Whitney - most recently of Hamden, Connecticut who, along with others in Connecticut, made real the idea of mass-producing interchangeable parts. Beyond his well-known cotton gin, Whitney was one of the first to utilize waterpower to run a factory where line shafts and belt-driven machine tools were utilized to mass produce on HIS assembly line muskets for a conflict that never really became a war with France. Now, Elon Musk on the shoulders of Benz, Whitney, Ford, and Nicola Tesla has advanced the idea of the car to what IT is today. Whitney built approximately 1,200 muskets for the war, falling short of his 10,000-unit contract. Even so, with others doing similar things, Whitney helped change the world of manufacturing forever. Now, Musk can build well over 1,000 TESLA Electric Cars in just ONE DAY. We've come a long way, baby.

Henry Ford's Model T - ESLA?

Not unlike Mr. Benz and his invention of the original horseless carriage, the Bechtells originally invented Pickle-pong, Pickle-ball, or sometimes simply Pickle. By making the game popular and available, the Pritchards, Bells, and McCallums, like Henry Ford, were granted the recognition and credit for the actual invention, another case of the conflation of invention and marketing, with a little R&D thrown in. Like Musk with his TESLA has taken cars, the USA Pickleball Association (USAPA) and others have taken Pickleball to where it is today and to where it will go tomorrow. Here's to their work, offering them all credit, with my full respect, GO TEAM! However, I was taught to always give credit where credit is due. There are many cases of mis- and dis-placed credit throughout history and society. By naming his car the TESLA, Mr. Musk credited Nicola as his inspiration, if nothing else. Good on you, Elon.

Between drinks, smokes, and battleships, the Bechtells entertained many guests at their island home north of Bainbridge, including one Joel Pritchard (R), member Washington State House of Representatives.

By virtue of his far greater name recognition and political successes, Mr. Pritchard, combined with Mr. Bell, and Mr. McCallum and his business acumen, have been mistakenly credited with the "invention" of Pickleball. In truth, its birthplace and early history lie a few miles to the north of Bainbridge Island, at a small home on the water's edge near the Mukilteo Ferry's point of disembarkation on the island of Whidbey.

Mr. Pritchard would become a bright light in the politics of Washington State and D.C. as well. Among many other good things, Mr. Pritchard's diligent work brought to legalization the "mother's right to choose", making Washington one of the first states in the U.S. to support this fundamental women's right. Later, Mr. Pritchard held a Senate seat, was part of the Watergate hearings, and with some help, formalized the game of Pickleball. While Mr. Pritchard and some friends clearly established the early "official game", credit for its genesis truly belongs elsewhere.

The Pritchards lived on Bainbridge, a goodly boat ride to the south of Whidbey. In the first version of the fledgling sport, the Bechtells managed to spawn a yard game that was a crude mix of badminton and ping-pong with a dash of tennis, using Wiffle balls and nets that were all liberated from between the yard darts and horse shoes in their cluttered and dank summer game and tool shed. This was the first iteration of Pickleball, perhaps discovered by Mr. Pritchard during a fundraising visit to my father's family summer home, twenty-five miles and a few years north of Bainbridge ...

After a long, long trip from there to here
Mount Rainier at dusk
on the quiet ferry ride
home ...

Fourteen

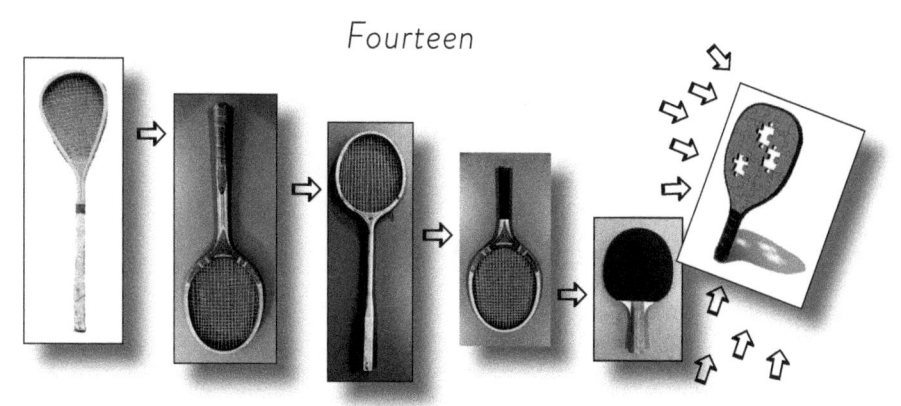

Sphairistike to Tennis to Pickleball

Current Court Dimensions and other Interesting Statistics

After the Pritchards and their friends moved Pickleball to their tennis court, the tennis net height carried over for a while but then was reset lower to improve the bounce option of the hard-court surface. Today the standard setting is thirty-six inches high on the ends, thirty-four inches high at center court. By comparison, tennis nets are forty-two inches high on the ends and thirty-six inches at center court.

The original Sphairistike (German Ball Playing) had an hourglass-shaped court, wide at the baseline and narrower at the net. The German game was modified and renamed Lawn Tennis by Major Walter Wingfield in 1873. The new court dimensions established by the Major have remained unchanged since their inception.

Today's tennis court is seventy-eight feet long with a width of twenty-seven feet for singles' matches and thirty-six feet for doubles', with the service line being twenty-one feet from the net.

Due to slower ball speeds and the shorter travel distance of the Pickleball itself, the court size was necessarily reduced on all sides to the dimensions that are closer to the size of my aunt's side yard than they are a tennis court. Standardized Pickleball court dimensions are only twenty feet wide and forty-four feet long, for both singles' and doubles' matches, a very manageable area of play for Pickleballers of all ages. The Non-Volley Zone at Center Court - The Kitchen - extends seven feet on either side of the net. One should not play much in the Kitchen because glasses will become broken in the sink, and the hostess will not be pleased! I tend to think that if Center Court is called The Kitchen, then the outer borderline of the court should be called the Rose Line, in honor of Aunt Gretchen's thorny throne, my personal nod to filial piety.

... Never Say Never ... Go For It!

Fifteen

The Sound ~ Unique

People gravitate toward sight, smell, and sound. Various combinations of these elements exist in everything we do. Both tennis balls and Pickleballs have a very pleasing sound when struck with strong intention. The tennis ball "poik" and the Pickleball "thwok" are a significant and attractive feature of both games.

As I mentioned earlier, even if Henry Ford had invented the car in the United States, by extension, he did not invent the Tesla. By today's standards, contemporary Pickleball far outstrips the modest, sodden, repurposing of damp and tattered casual sporting equipment developed by my father's side of the family. Their side yard and tattered paddles have given way to the PickleMaster court surface with $200 graphite paddles and 26- to 40-holed fully recyclable #4 Low Density Polyethylene balls available in a rainbow of colors. The balls were once made in my transplant home state of Connecticut; now they are made in China. The kitchen is no longer only in the house, where one may refresh a gimlet.

According to www.Tenniscoach.com, tennis 2nd serves for women average approximately 82 mph, while men's 2nd serves average 93 mph.

Conversely, www.jbrish.com observes that in Pickleball volleys at the Kitchen line, skill notwithstanding, ball velocity due to the aerodynamic limitations of a 0.8 ounce Pickleball dictate that the fastest non-gender specific Pickleball spike would top out at 40 mph, with volleys averaging closer to 25mph. Isaac Newton would love this game!

Because of the slower mental and physical reaction times required of Pickleballers, mixed teams of gender and age are suddenly possible, the only determiners of success being skill level and practice. Pickleball is universally accessible and literally levels the playing field for anyone and everyone from age 6 to 106. On Frye Island, I have seen it all - grandparents playing with grandchildren and teens with toddlers. Casual, laughing matches are common - if you can stand and move, you can play. Contests that pit the top players in heated competition take place several times throughout the summer season of outdoor play. If you can't stand the heat, stay out of the Kitchen!

One last point, avoid walking around the court perimeter while the game is on. It is considered poor form, rude, and you will be roundly scolded for it! Been There ... Done That.

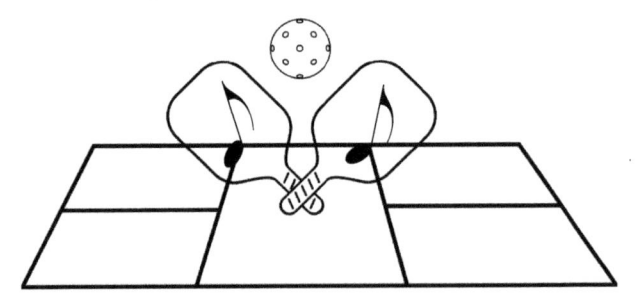

Closing

After moving back East as a young adult, going to school, getting married, having kids, and creating vacation traditions, I once again heard from friends on Frye Island about Pickleball as a fast-growing attraction on the Island's agenda of summer activities. Surprised by its growth and my personal connection to it beginnings, I decided I should write for you, the Pickle-ballers of the 21st century, the true yet unofficial story of this wonderful pastime.

Hope you enjoyed it because … it is all true. Play on, stay out of The Kitchen, and please … pass the Gherkins.

Afterword

When Patrick recalled his childhood memories, witnessing his family playing this new game, it was clear he had a story to share.

It is incredible and a bit surreal to consider that his bloodlines connect to the beginnings of a sport that now takes on such a life of its own. To say it has worldwide popularity does not express how much the game means to so many.

Little did the Bechtells, Bells, McCallums, Pritchards, Evans, and the rest of the gang ever fathom that this would one day evolve into the "fastest growing sport" in the United States and beyond!

We hope you enjoyed reading this book and will include it as part of a now known chapter in the history of this game. It was crafted with much care, some sweat, and even some tears.

This story relates to part of Patrick's early childhood. While his Pickleballing relatives have all gone to spirit, perhaps this telling of the evolution of Pickleball, along with Patrick's bringing forth this book serves as a loving recognition of their lives and their connection to the legacy of the sport of Pickleball.

With heart and much gratitude,

~ Melinda

Frye Island Dusk

~ WELCOME TO THE KITCHEN ~

Gretchen's Gherkins ...
NOT FOR THE FAINT OF HEART!

Start to Finish: About 4 days
What you get: About 8 pints of the best gherkins anywhere!

5 quarts cucumbers (pickling cucumbers 1-1/2 to 3-inch long)
1/2 cup pickling salt
8 cups granulated sugar, divided
6 cups distilled white vinegar, divided
3/4 teaspoon turmeric
2 teaspoons celery seeds
2 teaspoons pickling spices
8 pieces cinnamon sticks (1-inch)
1/2 teaspoon fennel seed (optional, but good)
1 teaspoon vanilla extract (optional, but good)
   5th of Vodka (optional, but good)
   EpiPen injectors of Insulin and Glucagon (recommended)

Directions:
Wash cucumbers, stems/leaves removed. Use the smallest ones you can find!!!

DAY 1: Late afternoon, place cucumbers in large bowl and submerge in boiling water. Let stand 6 to 8 hours.

DAY 2: Midmorning, drain cucumbers and re-submerge in fresh boiling water. Let stand 6 hours.

Late afternoon, drain water again and add salt; re-submerge in fresh boiling water.

DAY 3, Part I: Midmorning, drain cucumbers; poke with fork. Set vanilla aside for now, then combine 3 cups of the sugar, 3 cups of the vinegar, herbs, and the remaining spices in a BIG pan. Heat just to a boil, then pour over cucumbers.

DAY 3, Part II: In the afternoon, drain syrupy mixture into a large container; add 2 more cups of sugar and 2 more cups of vinegar. Reheat to a boil and pour back over cucumbers. Cover and let stand.

DAY 4, Part I: Midmorning, drain syrupy mixture again into a BIG pan; add 2 cups MORE sugar and 1 more cup of vinegar. Reheat to boiling and pour back over pickles.

DAY 4, Part II: In the afternoon, prepare jars. Drain syrupy mixture back into a large container; add 1 final cup of sugar and NOW the vanilla extract to the mix; heat to boiling. Pack pickles snuggly into clean, hot jars. Cover with hot syrup, leaving 1/2 inch of head room in the jar, then seal it. Carefully submerge sealed jars in boiling water for 10 minutes. Remove and let cool.

If you haven't yet drunk any of the vodka, you are behind schedule. Keep EpiPens within easy reach.

No Pickleball party planner would be complete without the appropriate whistle wetters ...

Lugubrious Lubricating Libations
~ a la Bechtell

From the kitchen, "I need a DRINK..." Chesty Bickford, 1963

Uncle Chuck's in the Bag Vodka Tonic

Chemistry:

2 oz vodka of your choice

4 oz tonic water

1 - 2 lime wedges

Execution:

Fill a highball glass with ice. Pour vodka in glass (I like Ketel One). Top with tonic water (I use diet tonic water at home, no reason other than taste in the mix).

Squeeze lime wedge(s) over the drink, drop wedge(s) into drink, and lightly stir. Serve with a duffle of Gherkins.

Johnny's Neat

Chemistry:
8 oz Dimple Scotch

Execution:
Fill a highball glass with Scotch
Drink
Brood about life
Repeat
Enter Rehab, Hold the Gherkins

Chuck's Naughty Vodka Gimlet

Chemistry:
1½ oz vodka
¾ oz lime juice
3-4 lime slices

Execution:
Pour Stolichnaya Vodka (I prefer Ketel One) and lime juice into mixing glass, shake and strain into martini glass. Add 3 to 4 slices of lime. Serve with Gherkins.

Mothers Ruin - Gretchen's Gin Gimlet

Chemistry:
2 oz gin
3/4 oz fresh lime juice
3/4 oz simple syrup
Cucumber wheel or lime wedge, for garnish

Execution:
Fill a cocktail shaker with ice and pour in the gin, lime

juice, and simple syrup (sugar dissolved in water 1:1 ratio). Stir vigorously with a long cocktail spoon until very cold.

Strain into a chilled coupe or martini glass, or strain over a rocks glass filled with ice, depending on preference. Garnish with the cucumber wheel and serve immediately. Gherkins add just the right insult to this injury.

Erm's Cosmo

Chemistry:
Dash of cranberry juice
1½ oz vodka
½ oz orange liqueur
¼ oz lime juice
Slice of lime

Execution:
Add dash of cranberry juice; pour liquor, liqueur, and lime juice into mixing glass. Shake briskly and pour into martini glass. Add slice of lime to garnish. Yes, have Gherkins on hand.

Chesty's Old Fashioned

Chemistry:
2 dashes aromatic bitters
½ tsp sugar dissolved with water and bitters
1½ oz of bourbon
1 cherry
1 orange slice
1 lemon wedge

Execution:
Fill glass with ice. Add cherry, orange slice, and lemon wedge. Pour in bourbon. Serve in a rocks glass over ice. Gherkins are a must.

Bud's Screwdriver

Chemistry:
2 oz vodka
Freshly squeezed orange juice
Orange wedge

Execution:
Pour vodka and fresh orange juice into cocktail glass and stir. Add orange wedge. Serve Gherkins with caution… the OJ makes this a tough call.

Chesty's Upset Applecart

Chemistry:
1½ oz apple brandy
¾ oz Triple Sec
¾ oz fresh lemon juice
1 orange slice

Execution:
Put first three ingredients in mixing glass; shake briskly. Prepare sugar-rimmed snifter. Strain into glass and garnish with orange slice. Serve with Gherkins for a pleasant flavor shock.

Bechtell King Alphonse (White Russian)

Chemistry:
1 oz vodka
½ oz coffee liqueur
1 oz heavy cream

Execution:

Pour vodka, coffee liqueur, and heavy cream into cocktail glass. Stir well.

NO to the Gherkins on this one ... it curdles the cream.

Bechtell BM (Bloody Mary)

Chemistry:

1½ oz vodka
2 dashes Worcestershire sauce
1 tsp horseradish
Tomato or Clamato juice
4 dashes Tabasco sauce
Celery salt
Fresh ground pepper
Salt

Execution:

Put all ingredients in mixing glass; shake briskly. Pour into pint glass over ice. Add a celery branch to garnish. Avoid open flame. Serve with Gherkins.

Avuncular Vodka Martini (Uncle Chuck) aka The SST

Chemistry:

2½ oz vodka
1½ oz dry vermouth
3 green olives
Black pepper

Execution:

Rinse martini glass with dry vermouth and pour out. Shake

vodka with ice and a tiny pinch of freshly ground black pepper until chilled. Pour into martini glass, add olives, fly high.

Erminie's Rump Slappin' Dirty Martini
Attenzione: Shaken not Stirred

Chemistry:
2½ oz vodka
1½ oz dry vermouth
½ oz olive juice
3-4 green olives, stuffed with blue cheese

Execution:
Add dry vermouth to the martini glass, rinse, and pour out. Pour vodka, olive juice, and ice into mixing glass. Shaken not stirred until chilled. Strain into the martini glass and drop in the 3 to 4 olives as garnish; have slip and fall attorney at the ready.

Rainier Beer

Chemistry:
Rainier Beer Covers This Part
Execution: Store on ice
    Mow lawn at High Noon
        Sweat copiously
            Drink Rainier Beer ...
Ribbit, Ribbit, Ribbit, Ribbit, Rainier, *Ribbit,* Beer, *Ribbit, Ribbit, Rainier, Ribbit, Ribbit, Beer, ... You are now sufficiently Pickled!* ~ ps

A joke is only as good as its telling (Ribbit...) For the punchline,
Google: **Rainier Beer Frogs**

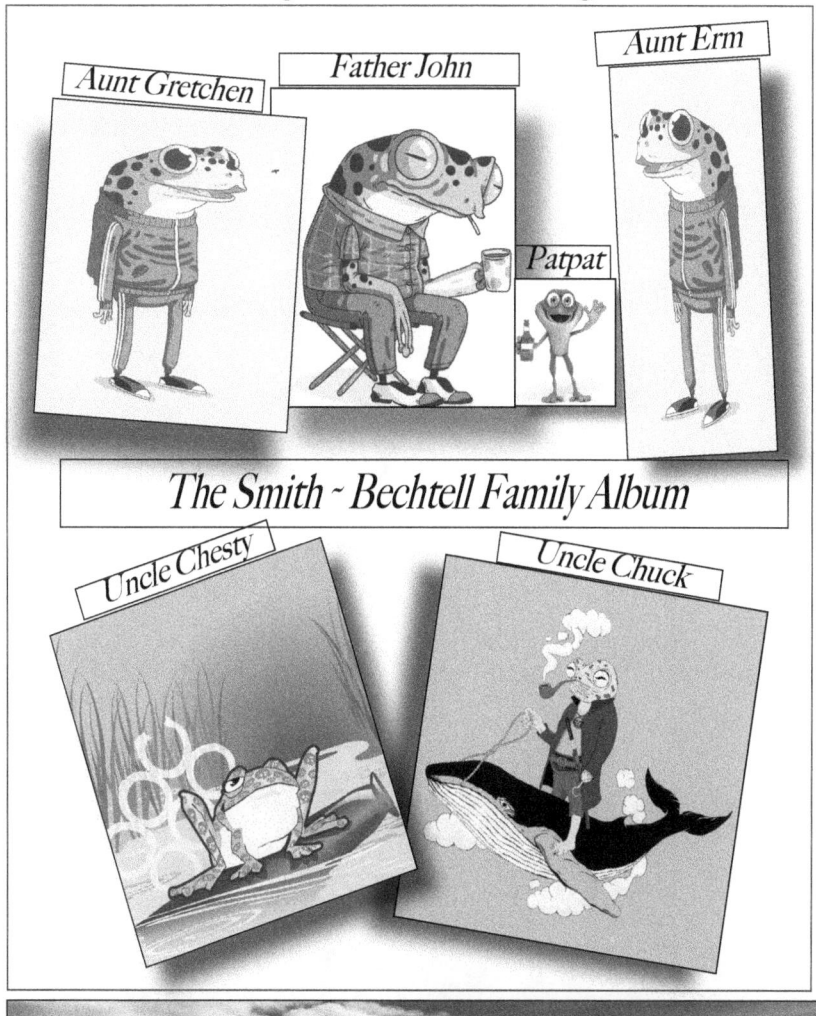

Aunt Gretchen

Father John

Aunt Erm

Patpat

The Smith ~ Bechtell Family Album

Uncle Chesty

Uncle Chuck

Quiet on the Lake

When enjoying a drink on the rocks, these are my preferred rocks.

Pat's Perfect Pickleball Party Planner
Recipes for a Pickled - Ball

With Pickleball being the fastest growing sport in America today, what better way to enjoy it than with a plan for a party in the style of the times in which Pickleball came to be?

Ambrosia Salad

(1) 15-ounce can mandarin oranges, drained
(1) 8-ounce can crushed pineapple, drained
1 cup maraschino cherries, drained
8 ounces green seedless grapes, cut in half
1 cup miniature marshmallows
1 cup sweetened shredded coconut
1 cup Miracle Whip, or to taste

Directions:
- In a large bowl, combine the oranges, pineapple, cherries, grapes, marshmallows, and coconut.
- Add Miracle Whip and toss to mix.
- Cover and refrigerate for several hours before serving.

Bacon-Wrapped Water Chestnuts

16 bacon strips
2 cans (8 ounces, each) whole water chestnuts, drained
1/3 cup ketchup
1/3 cup yellow mustard
1/4 cup maple syrup or brown sugar
1 garlic clove, minced
Wooden toothpicks

Directions:

• Preheat oven to 400° F. • Cut bacon strips crosswise in half. • In a large skillet, cook bacon over medium heat until partially cooked but not crisp. • Remove to paper towels to drain; keep warm.

• Wrap a bacon piece around each whole water chestnut. • Secure with a toothpick. • Place in a 15 x 10 x 1-inch ungreased baking pan. • Bake for 10 minutes. • In a bowl, combine ketchup, mustard, syrup (or brown sugar) and garlic; drizzle over bacon-wrapped water chestnuts. • Bake until bacon is crisp, about 10 minutes longer.

Cabezone

1-pound Italian pork sausage, casings removed
1 small yellow onion, chopped
2 eggs, lightly beaten
1/2 cup grated Swiss cheese
1/2 teaspoon garlic powder
salt and black pepper, to taste
2 - 1/4 cups Bisquick baking mix
2/3 cup milk

Directions:

- Sauté sausage in skillet until browned. Remove from pan.
- Sauté chopped yellow onions in same pan that includes sausage drippings.
- In bowl, mix browned sausage, softened onions, eggs, grated Swiss cheese, garlic powder, salt, and black pepper.
- In separate bowl, mix Bisquick baking mix with milk until combined.
- Combine sausage mixture with biscuit mixture.
- Spread mixture evenly in 13 x 9-inch baking dish that has been lightly greased.
- Bake in 400 ° F oven for approximately 20 minutes or until golden brown.
- Cool, cut into squares, serve.

Cheese Ball

1 package (8 ounces) cream cheese, softened
1 cup sharp cheddar, finely shredded
1 cup blue cheese or Gorgonzola, crumbled
1 teaspoon Worcestershire sauce
2 teaspoons garlic salt
1 teaspoon onion powder
1 tablespoon dried parsley
1/2 cup finely chopped pecans or walnuts, toasted (or 1/2 cup sesame seeds, lightly toasted)
Assorted crackers

Directions:
- Mix first seven ingredients in a bowl.
- Blend extremely well.
- Press ingredients together, removing air pockets.
- Shape into ball.
- Roll cheese ball in toasted nuts (or sesame seeds)
- Coat completely.
- Refrigerate until ready to serve.
- Serve with assorted crackers.

Clam Crisps

1 rib celery, finely minced
1 small yellow onion, finely minced
1 garlic clove, finely minced
Olive oil, enough to coat bottom of skillet
(4) 6.5-ounce cans minced clams, reserve liquid
1 teaspoon Worcestershire sauce
1/4 teaspoon crushed red pepper flakes
Pinch salt
1/2 cup (approximately) dry breadcrumbs
1-pound loaf white bread, crust trimmed
4 tablespoons salted butter, melted
Wooden toothpicks

Directions:
- Sauté onions and celery in olive oil until softened.
- Add garlic and cook until fragrant.
- To the skillet, add minced clams with their juices, Worcestershire sauce, crushed red pepper, and salt.
- Cook on medium heat for 3 – 5 minutes.
- To the skillet add enough breadcrumbs until the liquids have been absorbed and a moderately stiff paste is formed.
- Let the mixture cool. In the meantime, use a rolling pin to flatten each slice of bread.
- Place a scant teaspoon of clam mixture atop each bread slice and roll it, similar to a "burrito", encasing the clam mixture.
- Secure the roll in two places with toothpicks.

• Cut the roll in two pieces, with each piece having its own toothpick.

• Place clam rolls on parchment-lined baking sheet and brush with melted butter.

• Bake 400 ° F approximately 10 – 12 minutes, or until lightly browned.

Cucumber Canapes

1 cup mayonnaise
3 ounces cream cheese, softened
1 tablespoon grated yellow onion
1 tablespoon minced chives
1/2 teaspoon cider vinegar
1/2 teaspoon Worcestershire sauce
1 garlic clove, minced
1/4 teaspoon paprika
1/8 teaspoon curry powder
1/8 teaspoon each dried oregano, thyme, basil, parsley flakes and dill weed
1 loaf (1 pound) white or rye bread, crust trimmed
2 medium cucumbers, scored and thinly sliced
Diced pimientos and additional dill weed, for garnish

Directions:

• Combine the mayonnaise, cream cheese, onion, chives, vinegar, Worcestershire sauce, garlic, seasonings, and dried herbs. • Blend well. • Cover and refrigerate for 2 hours.

• Using a 2-1/2-inch biscuit cutter, cut out circles from bread slices. • Spread mayonnaise mixture over bread slices.

• Top with cucumber slices. • Garnish with pimientos and dill.

Deviled Eggs, with or without Gherkins

12 large eggs, hard-boiled and then peeled
1/2 cup mayonnaise, or to taste
1 tablespoon prepared mustard
1/4 cup sweet pickle relish, drained
1/4 teaspoon salt
dash white pepper
paprika, optional, but good
Gherkins, optional, and better!! After all, the game *was* named after them!

Directions:

• Slice eggs in half lengthwise and remove yolks; set whites aside. • In a small bowl, mash yolks. • Stir in mayonnaise,

mustard, pickle relish, salt, and pepper.
- Stuff or pipe mixture into egg whites.
- If desired, sprinkle with paprika.

Ham Salad Sliders

3/4 cup mayonnaise
1/2 cup finely chopped celery
1/4 cup sliced green onions
1 tablespoon honey
2 teaspoons spicy brown mustard
1/2 teaspoon Worcestershire sauce
1/4 teaspoon seasoned salt
5 cups finely diced fully cooked ham
1/3 cup chopped almonds, toasted
Slider buns, split

Directions:

- Mix first 7 ingredients. Stir in ham. Refrigerate, covered, until serving.
- Stir in almonds just before serving.
- Serve on buns.

Italian Pinwheels

1 tube (8 ounces) refrigerated crescent rolls

1/3 cup prepared pesto sauce

1/4 cup jarred, roasted sweet red peppers, drained and chopped

1/4 cup grated Parmesan cheese

1 cup pizza sauce, warmed

Directions:
- Unroll crescent dough into two long rectangles.
- Seal seams and perforations. • Spread each with pesto sauce. • Sprinkle each with red peppers and Parmesan cheese.
- Roll up each jelly-roll style, starting with a short side.
- With a sharp knife, cut each roll into 10 slices.
- Place cut side down 2 inches apart on two parchment-lined baking sheets.
- Bake at 400° F until golden brown, 8-10 minutes.
- Serve warm with pizza sauce.

Notes: *What did I forget??? ... Relax, these are just DUMP recipes after all! ... Ah, I remember ...*

... I'm not DRINKING enough!

Mushroom Stuffed Tomatoes

Cherry tomatoes, 24 in number
1/4 teaspoon salt
1 pound sliced fresh mushrooms, finely chopped
1/4 cup salted butter
2 tablespoons all-purpose flour
1 cup half-and-half cream
2 tablespoons soft breadcrumbs
1/4 cup minced fresh parsley
2/3 cup shredded cheddar cheese, divided

Directions:

• Cut tomatoes in half; scoop out and discard pulp, leaving a thin shell. • Sprinkle lightly with salt; invert on paper towels to drain for 15 minutes.

• In a large skillet, sauté mushrooms in butter until most of the liquid has evaporated, about 5 minutes. • Sprinkle with flour; stir in cream. • Bring to a boil; cook and stir until thickened, about 2 minutes.

• Remove from the heat. • Stir in the breadcrumbs, parsley, and 1/3 cup of cheese. • Spoon mixture into tomato cups. Sprinkle with remaining cheese.

• Place in a lightly greased 13x9-inch baking dish. • Bake, uncovered, at 400°F until cheese is melted, about 10 minutes.

Nonni's Olive-Stuffed Celery

1 dill pickle spear, plus 1 teaspoon juice
3 sweet pickles, plus 1 teaspoon juice
6 pitted black olives, plus 1 teaspoon juice
6 pimiento-stuffed olives, plus 1 teaspoon juice
1 package (8 ounces) cream cheese, softened
1/3 cup Miracle Whip
Pinch salt
1/4 cup finely chopped pecans or walnuts, toasted
6 celery ribs, cut into 2-inch pieces

Directions:

• Finely chop the pickles and olives; set aside. • In a small bowl, beat the cream cheese, Miracle Whip, juices, and salt until blended. • Stir in the pickles, olives, and nuts.

• Pipe or stuff filling into celery sticks. • Refrigerate until firm.

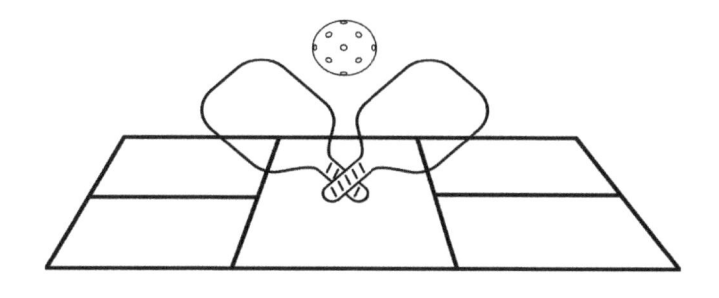

Oysters Rockefeller

1 medium onion, finely chopped
1/2 cup unsalted butter, cubed
1 package (9 ounces) fresh spinach, torn
1 cup grated Romano cheese
1 tablespoon lemon juice
1/8 teaspoon black pepper
3 dozen fresh oysters in the shell, washed
2 pounds kosher salt

Directions:

• In a large skillet, sauté onion in butter until tender. • Add spinach; cook and stir until wilted. • Remove from the heat; stir in cheese, lemon juice, and black pepper.

• Spread kosher salt onto 2 ungreased 15x10x1-in. baking pans. • Shuck oysters, reserving oyster and its liquid in bottom shell. • Lightly press oyster shells into the bed of salt, using salt to keep oysters level in the baking pan. • Top each oyster with 2-1/2 teaspoons spinach mixture.

• Bake, uncovered, at 450° F until oysters are plump, 6-8 minutes. • Serve immediately.

Salmon Mousse Cucumber Canapes

2 English cucumbers
1 package (8 ounces) cream cheese, softened
1/2-pound smoked salmon
1 tablespoon whole milk
1 teaspoon lemon-pepper seasoning
1 teaspoon snipped fresh dill
salt and pepper to taste
1/2 cup heavy whipping cream
additional snipped fresh dill, garnish

Directions:
- Peel strips from cucumbers to create a decorative edge; cut cucumbers into 1/2-inch slices. • Using a melon baller, remove a small amount of cucumber from the center of each slice, leaving the bottom intact.
- Place the cream cheese, smoked salmon, milk, lemon pepper, and dill in a food processor. • Cover and process until blended. • Transfer to a small bowl and season with salt and pepper. • In another bowl, beat heavy cream until stiff peaks form. • Fold into salmon mixture.
- Pipe or dollop mousse onto cucumber slices; garnish with dill. • Refrigerate until ready to serve.

Pickleball Party Archival Classics ~ The Coronary Collection

Cheese Dreams
Cheese Bread from the 1950s

8 oz cream cheese

1 jar Old English cheese { Kraft Cheese Spread }

1 stick oleo margarine

• leave at room temp and whip with a electric beater till fluffy

• arrange 1 loaf white bread in stacks of 3 slices and spread with cheese { mixture }. Trim crust.

• cut into 3rds and frost the outside with cheese mixture { can be frozen }

• heat in 400° F oven till bubbly and lightly browned

Notes & Substitutions:_____
_____
_____
_____.

Noodle Nibbles
Self-explanatory

3 tablespoons oleo	1 can chow mein noodles
2 teaspoons soy sauce	1/4 teaspoon celery salt
4 drops hot sauce	dash onion powder

- combine melted oleo, soy sauce, and hot pepper sauce
- drizzle over chow mein noodles and toss till well coated
- sprinkle noodles with celery salt and onion powder
- toast in 275° F oven for 12 to 15 minutes or till lightly browned

YIELD 2 1/2 cups

Notes & Substitutions:

Sour Cream Jello Appetizer
on that special occasion when only the best will do ~

- dissolve 1 package unflavored gelatin in 1/4 cup boiling water
- add 1/2 cup old water and stir well
- add 2 cups sour cream and mix until *smooth*
- add 1/8 teaspoon cayenne pepper or hot sauce
- add 1/8 teaspoon salt
- add 1 teaspoon Worchestershire sauce
- mix well, pour into mold, and chill

   ~ good with dabs of red caviar in bottom of the mold

Notes & Substitutions:_____
_____
_____
_____.

More Notes:

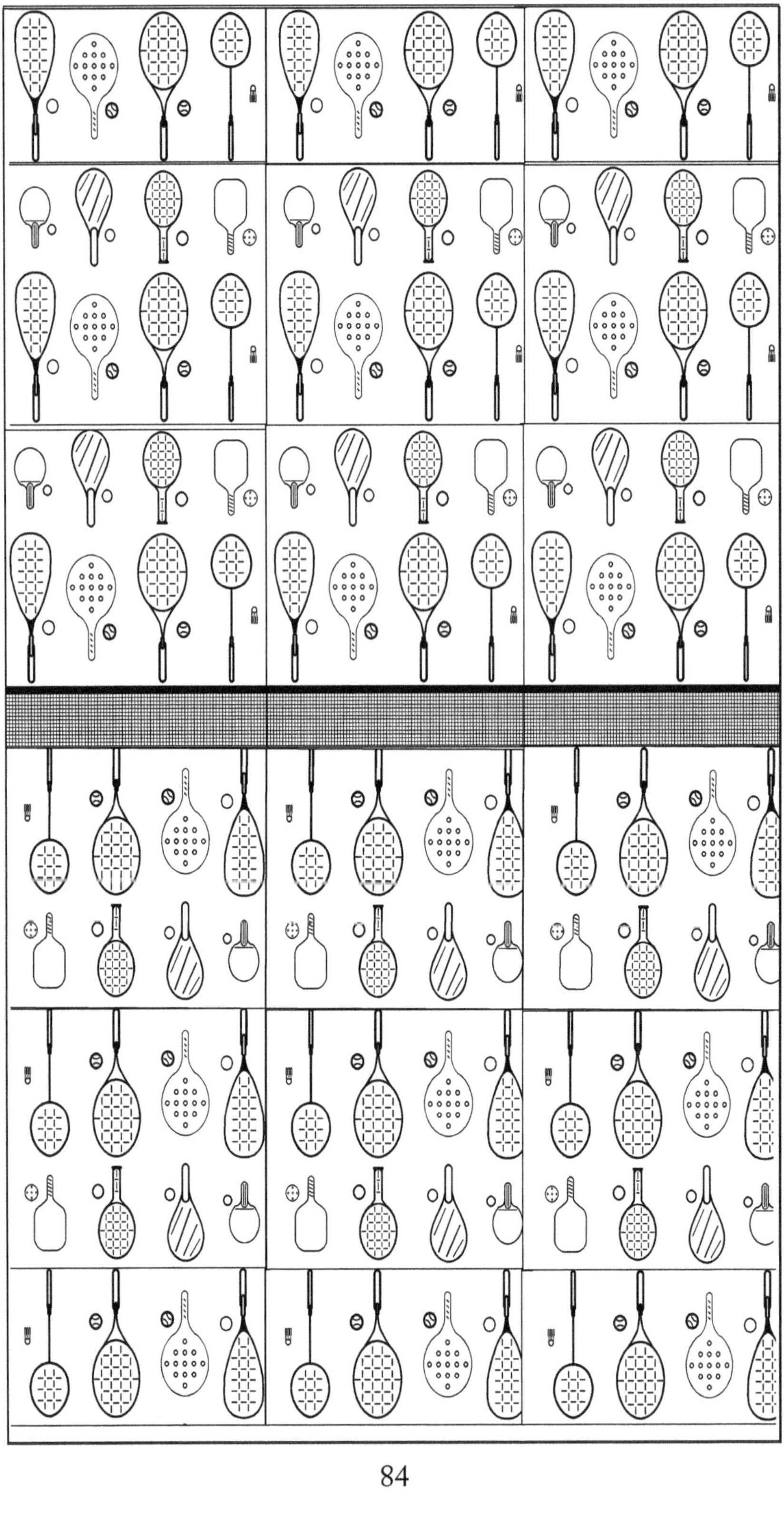

Appendix One
"Injustice Anywhere is a Threat to Justice Everywhere" - MLK

Chief Seattle's Speech and Letter to The "Big Chief at Washington", President Franklin Pierce

"Yonder sky that has wept tears of compassion upon my people for centuries untold, and which to us appears changeless and eternal, may change. Today is fair. Tomorrow it may be overcast with clouds. My words are like the stars that never change. Whatever Seattle says, the great chief at Washington can rely upon with as much certainty as he can upon the return of the sun or the seasons. The white chief says that Big Chief at Washington sends us greetings of friendship and goodwill. This is kind of him for we know he has little need of our friendship in return. His people are many. They are like the grass that covers vast prairies. My people are few. They resemble the scattering trees of a stormswept plain. The great, and I presume -- good, White Chief sends us word that he wishes to buy our land but is willing to allow us enough to live comfortably. This indeed appears just, even generous, for the Red Man no longer has rights that he need respect, and the offer may be wise, also, as we are no longer in need of an extensive country.

There was a time when our people covered the land as the waves of a wind-ruffled sea cover its shell-paved floor, but that time long since passed away with the greatness of tribes that are now but a mournful memory. I will not dwell

George Custer and his map of tribal lands and military posts. Drawn in 1874, two years before his death at Little Bighorn, Montana. Harper's Weekly, pg. 691 August 22, 1874

on, nor mourn over, our untimely decay, nor reproach my paleface brothers with hastening it, as we too may have been somewhat to blame.

Youth is impulsive. When our young men grow angry at some real or imaginary wrong, and disfigure their faces with black paint, it denotes that their hearts are black, and that they are often cruel and relentless, and our old men and old women are unable to restrain them. Thus it has ever been. Thus it was when the white man began to push our forefathers ever westward. But let us hope that the hostilities between us may never return. We would have everything to lose and nothing to gain. Revenge by young men is considered gain, even at the cost of their own lives, but old men who stay at home in times of war, and mothers who have sons to lose, know better.

Our good father in Washington--for I presume he is now our father as well as yours, since King George has moved his boundaries further north--our great and good father, I say, sends us word that if we do as he desires he will protect us. His brave warriors will be to us a bristling wall of strength, and his wonderful ships of war will fill our harbors, so that our ancient enemies far to the northward -- the Haidas and Tsimshians -- will cease to frighten our women, children, and old men. Then in reality he will be our father and we his children. But can that ever be? Your God is not our God! Your God loves your people and hates mine! He folds his strong protecting arms lovingly about the paleface and leads him by the hand as a father leads an infant son. But, He has forsaken His Red children, if they really are His. Our God, the Great Spirit, seems also to have forsaken us. Your God makes your people wax stronger every day. Soon they will fill all the land. Our people are ebbing away like a rapidly receding tide that will never return. The white man's God cannot love our people or He would protect them. They seem to be orphans who can look nowhere for help. How then can we be brothers? How can your God become our God and renew our prosperity and awaken in us dreams of returning greatness? If we have a common Heavenly Father He must be partial, for He came to His paleface children. We never saw Him. He gave you laws but had no word for His red children whose teeming multitudes once filled this vast continent as stars fill the firmament. No; we are two distinct races with separate origins and separate destinies. There is little in common between us.

To us the ashes of our ancestors are sacred and their resting place is hallowed ground. You wander far from the graves of your ancestors and seemingly without regret. Your religion was written upon tablets of stone by the iron finger of your God so that you could not forget. The Red Man could never comprehend or remember it. Our religion is the traditions of our ancestors -- the dreams of our old men, given them in solemn hours of the night by the Great Spirit; and the visions of our sachems, and is written in the hearts of our people.

Your dead cease to love you and the land of their nativity as soon as they pass the portals of the tomb and wander away beyond the stars. They are soon forgotten and never return. Our dead never forget this beautiful world that gave them being. They still love its verdant valleys, its murmuring rivers, its magnificent mountains, sequestered vales and verdant lined lakes and bays, and ever yearn in tender fond affection over the lonely hearted living, and often return from the happy hunting ground to visit, guide, console, and comfort them.

Day and night cannot dwell together. The Red Man has ever fled the approach of the White Man, as the morning mist flees before the morning sun. However, your proposition seems fair and I think that my people will accept it and will retire to the reservation you offer them. Then we will dwell apart in peace, for the words of the Great White Chief seem to be the words of nature speaking to my people out of dense darkness.

It matters little where we pass the remnant of our days. They will not be many. The Indian's night promises to be dark. Not a single star of hope hovers above his horizon. Sad-voiced winds moan in the distance. Grim fate seems to be on the Red Man's trail, and wherever he will hear the approaching footsteps of his fell destroyer and prepare stolidly to meet his doom, as does the wounded doe that hears the approaching footsteps of the hunter.

A few more moons, a few more winters, and not one of the descendants of the mighty hosts that once moved over this broad land or lived in happy homes, protected by the Great Spirit, will remain to mourn over the graves of a people once more powerful and hopeful than yours. But why should I mourn at the untimely fate of my people? Tribe follows tribe, and nation follows nation, like the waves of the sea. It is the order of nature, and regret is useless. Your time of decay may be distant, but it will surely come, for even the White Man whose God walked and talked with him as friend to friend, cannot be exempt from the common destiny. We may be brothers after all. We will see.

We will ponder your proposition and when we decide we will let you know. But should we accept it, I here and now make this condition that we will not be denied the privilege without molestation of visiting at any time the tombs of our ancestors, friends, and children. Every part of this soil is sacred in the estimation of my people. Every hillside, every valley, every plain and grove, has been hallowed by some sad or happy event in days long vanished. Even the rocks, which seem to be dumb and dead as the swelter in the sun along the silent shore, thrill with memories of stirring events connected with the lives of my people, and the very dust upon which you now stand responds more lovingly to their footsteps than yours, because it is rich with the blood of our ancestors, and our bare feet are conscious of the sympathetic touch. Our departed braves, fond mothers, glad, happy hearted maidens, and even the little children who lived here and rejoiced here for a brief season, will love these somber solitudes and at eventide they greet shadowy returning spirits. And when the last Red Man shall have perished, and the memory of my tribe shall have become a myth among the White Men, these shores will swarm with the invisible dead of my tribe, and when your children's children think themselves alone in the field, the store, the shop, upon the highway, or in the silence of the pathless woods, they will not be alone. In all the earth there is no place dedicated to solitude. At night when the streets of your cities and villages are silent and you think them deserted, they will throng with the returning hosts that once filled them and still love this beautiful land. The White Man will never be alone.

Let him be just and deal kindly with my people, for the dead are not powerless. Dead, did I say? There is no death, only a change of worlds.

>   from "The Nomadic Spirit", where this is version 1.
>   (Google: *The Nomadic Spirit's Chief Seattle Resources*
>   for the historical debate over various versions of this speech)

~ ~ ~

Chief Seattle, 1780 - 1866 The name "Seattle" is an anglicised version of Si'ahl. Chief Si'ahl, most likely due to this letter and speech, is the most famous of the known Duwamish Chiefs. His mother was Duwamish but his father was a Chief of the Suquamish Tribe. As Chief, Si'ahl centralized his power to include several other local tribes. For several millennia they all shared hunting and fishing lands in relative peace before George Vancouver entered the equation.

Ancient fishing waters as they look today

*Bust of Chief Seattle, Renton, Washington, July 7, 1936,
Courtesy of the Seattle Municipal Archives - 10641*

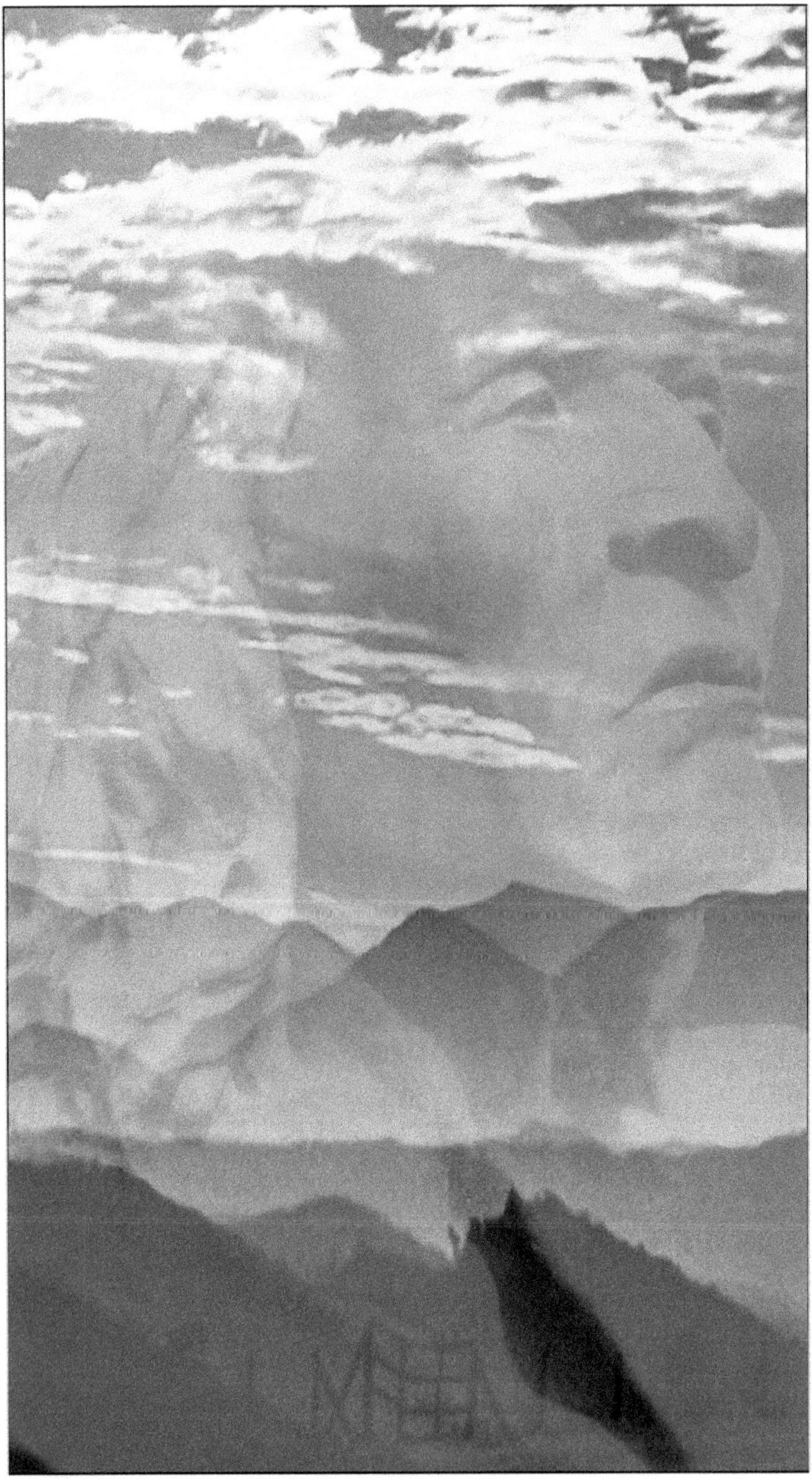

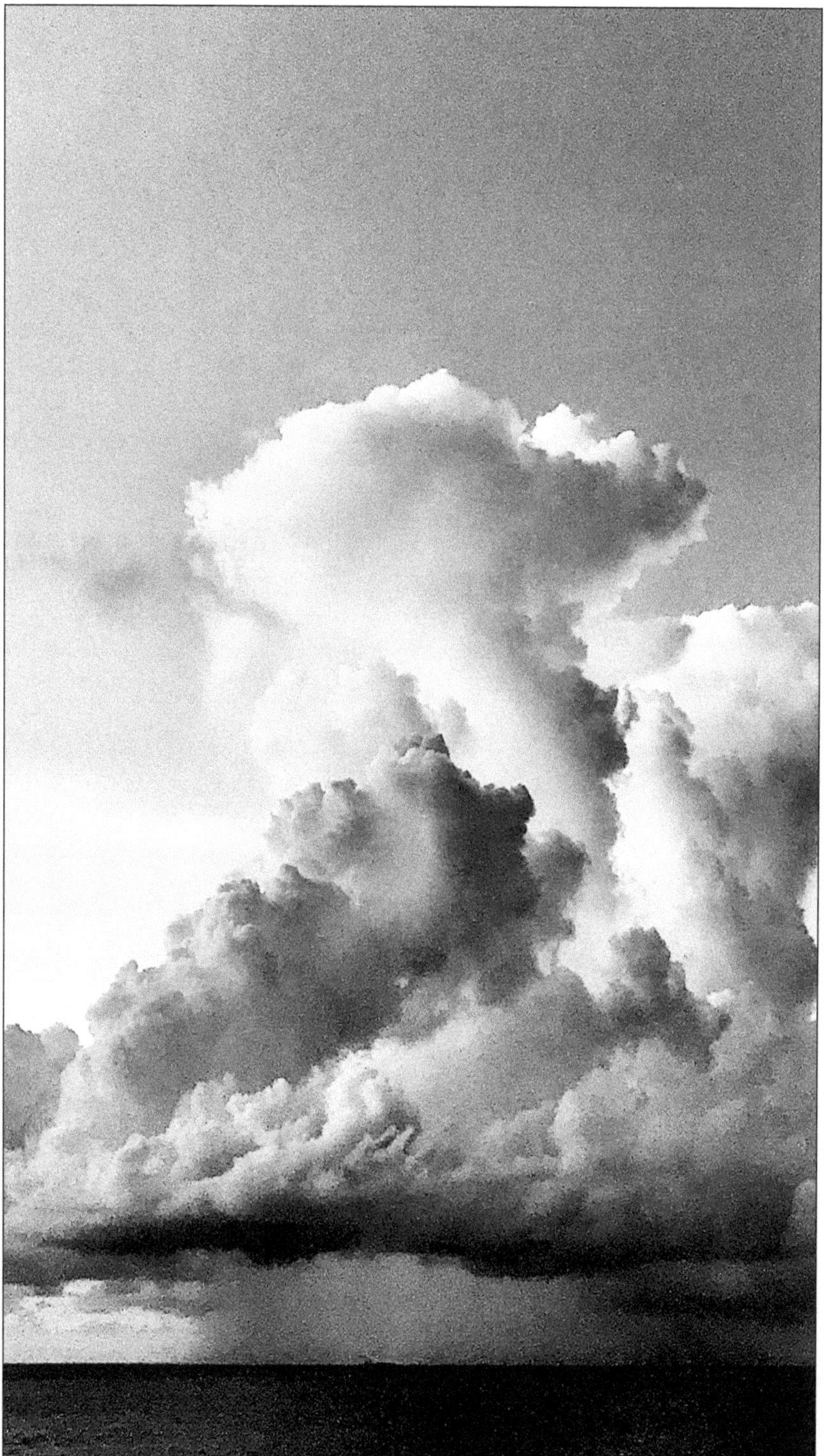

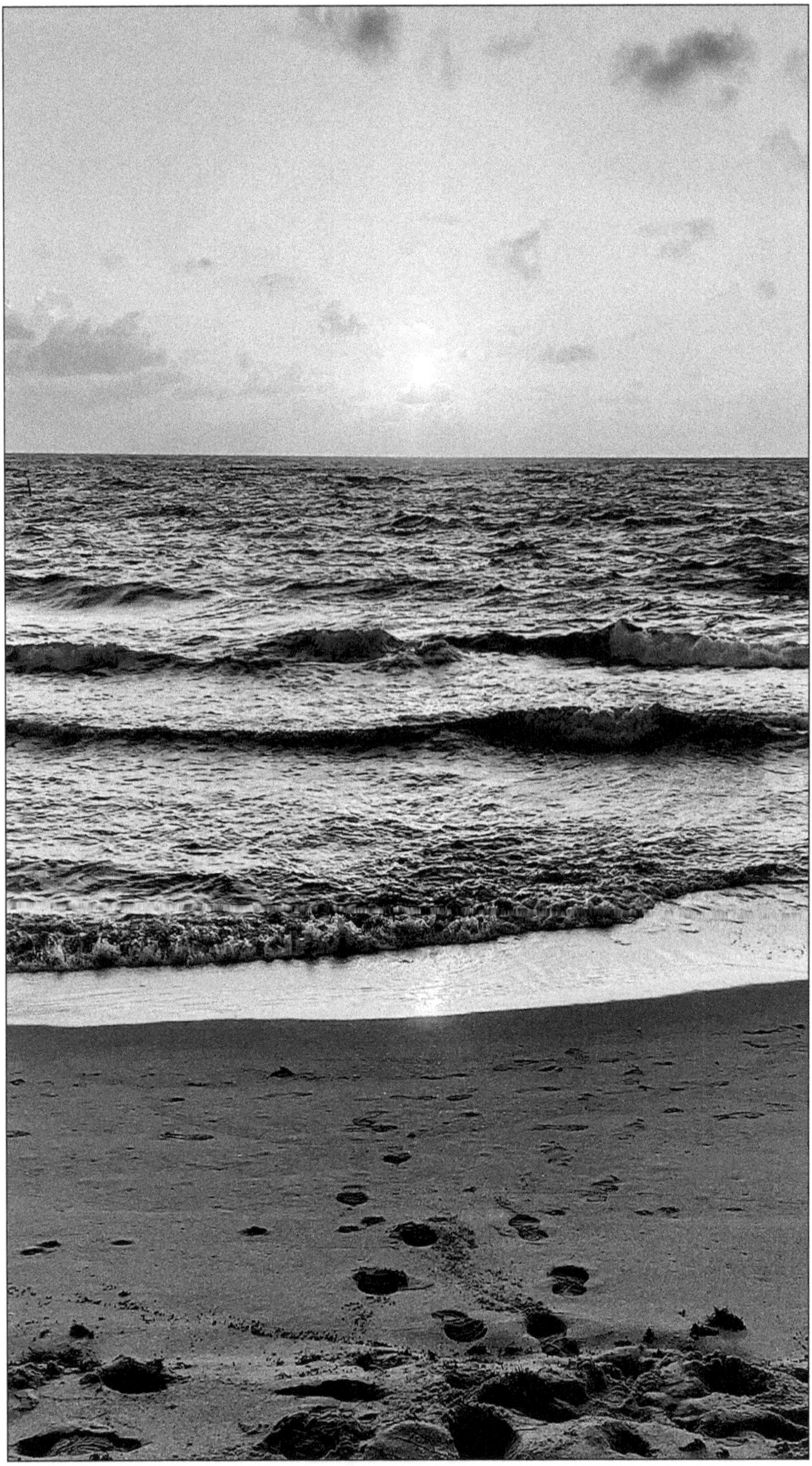

Appendix Two

Pickleball Terminology Past & Present and the Current Rules from *Pickleball USA*

"Now *That's* How you Pepper a Steak!" –
from an NPR interview, Pickleball Enthusiast Owen Wilson, American actor

The Expanding Lexicon of Pickleball Phrasiology

Thanks to *pinkpickleball.com, amazinaces.com, onixpickleball.com*

ACE: A serve that is not returned by the opposing team.

APPROACH SHOT: The ball is hit while moving forward towards the Pickleball net.

BACKHAND: Moving the paddle back to prepare for a shot.

BACKSPIN: Hitting the ball with a low to high motion that causes the ball to spin in the opposite direction.

BOUNCE IT: Partner calls this when the ball is likely to land out of bounds.

CARRY: Hitting the ball in such a way that it does not bounce away from the Pickleball paddle but tends to be carried along on the face of the paddle during its forward motion.

CROSS-COURT: The court diagonally opposite your court.

CROSS-COURT DINK: This is a dink that carries all the way from one side of the court to the other and usually lands in the opposite opponent's non-volley zone, "The Kitchen". (Uncle Chuck's "South Paw", the very first ever Cross-court Dink?)

Dead Ball: The term used to describe the Pickleball ball after a fault is declared, or when the ball has gone out and the current point is over.

Dink Shot: A soft shot that is intended to arc over the Pickleball net and land within the non-volley zone.

Double Bounce: A ball that bounces more than once, on one side, before it is returned. Following the serve, each side must make at least one ground stroke, prior to volleying the ball (hitting it out of the air).

Drop Shot: A groundstroke shot that falls short of the opponent's position.

Drop Shot Volley: A volley shot that is designed to "kill" the speed of the ball and return it short, near the net.

Face of the Paddle: The surface of the paddle used to make shots.

Falafel: No, not the Middle Eastern food! A falafel in Pickleball is a shot that doesn't reach its full potential, due to the player hitting the ball without any power.

Fault: A fault is any action that stops play because of a rule violation.

First Serve: To begin a new game, only one partner from the first serving side is allowed to serve. After the first fault, the serve switches to the opposing side.

Flapjack: A shot that must bounce once before it can be hit.

Foot Fault: An illegal serve or volley because of foot placement.

Forehand: Forehand shot hit on a player's dominant side. For example for a left-handed player, a ball hit on the left side.

Groundstroke: Hitting the ball after one bounce.

HALF VOLLEY: A groundstroke shot where the paddle contacts the ball immediately after it bounces from the court and before the ball rises to its potential height.

HINDER: Any element or occurrence that affects play.

KITCHEN: Slang term for the Non-Volley Zone. As in, "Stay out of the…!" *See page 31 final paragraph for specific usage.*

LET: A serve that hits the net cord and lands in the service court. Let also may refer to a rally that must be replayed for any reason.

LINE CALL: Calling the ball in or out.

LINE CALLS: If any part of the ball lands on the court lines, it is considered "in" (except in the case of the Non-Volley Zone line).

LOB: A shot that returns the ball as high and deep as possible, forcing the opposing side back to the baseline, the backcourt, thus making the opponent run for the ball and lose position.

NICE GET: If someone on the court yells "nice get", this means that a difficult ball was reached or returned.

NICE RALLY: This is a compliment to all players, meaning there has been a long streak of shots between teams.

NICE SETUP: This is another compliment. In Pickleball, a setup means one player has successfully manipulated another player to move to an area of the court that leaves an exposed section not covered by the opposing team.

NON-VOLLEY ZONE ("THE KITCHEN"): The section of court adjacent to the net. A player cannot volley a ball while standing within the non-volley zone. It includes all lines surrounding the zone.

OPA!: A cheer shouted after the third shot has been hit and open rallying has started.

Overhead shot: A shot hit over the shoulder, similar to a tennis serve.

Overhead Slam / Smash: A hard overhand shot, usually resulting from an opponent's lob, high return, or high bounce.

Passing Shot: A volley or groundstroke shot that is aimed at a distance from the player and is designed to prevent return of the ball.

Pickle!: A player shouts "Pickle!" to let the other players know that a serve is coming.

Pickled: If a team fails to score by the end of the game, the team has been pickled. This is to be avoided.

Pickledome: The court where the championship match in a Pickleball tournament is played.

Pickler: Someone who is obsessed with Pickleball and cannot stop talking about the sport. Are you a Pickleball addict?

Poach: Poaching is when one team member takes the shot going towards a partner, instead of letting the partner play.

Punch: A quick shot with a minimal backswing, with a similar motion to stabbing the ball out of the air with the paddle.

Put away: A ball that the opponent cannot return, therefore a winning shot.

Rally: Continuous play that occurs after the serve and before a fault.

Replays: Any rallies that are replayed for any reason, without the awarding of a point or a side out.

Second Serve: A term used to describe the condition when a serving team begins the game or subsequently loses the first of its two allocated serves.

SERVE: An underhanded shot that begins a Pickleball rally. In Pickleball, you get two serves. The player must serve the ball from below the waist level.

SERVER NUMBER: If playing doubles, the server must call either "1" or "2", to identify who served first or second. This number must be called out along with the score.

SERVICE COURT: The area on either side of the centerline, bounded by the non-volley zone line, the baseline, and the sideline. All lines are included in the service court, except the non-volley zone line.

SERVICE OUTSIDE SCORING: In Pickleball, a player must get the serve to win a point and can only get a point while serving.

SIDE OUT: A side out is declared after one side loses its service, and the other side is awarded service.

SLAMMERS: Slammers hit the ball hard and fast. Advanced players claim that playing like this demonstrates poor technique as they can run out of energy quickly.

TOP SPIN: A shot with spin, caused by hitting the ball swinging low to high. Some Pickleball players buy a Pickleball paddle specifically for spin.

VOLLEY: Hitting the ball in the air, during a rally, before the ball has a chance to bounce onto the court.

VOLLEY LLAMA: An illegal move where a player hits a shot into "The Kitchen".

VOLLEY SHOT: This shot picks the ball out of the air before it bounces. This move is not allowed when the player is in the non-volley zone.

New Pickleball Terms

As if there weren't enough Pickleball terms to wrap your head around already, each year sees the arrival of several new words and phrases.

These new expressions are usually Pickleball sayings that have become popular on courts, but weren't previously official.

We will keep this section up-to-date with the new Pickleball terminology that gets added each year, so make sure you check back in 2023 to quickly get clued in!

New terms for 2022

Several changes were made to the Pickleball rules in 2022.

Here are the main changes to the Pickleball terms that came into effect:

TECHNICAL WARNING: A referee's warning for a behavioral violation. Points are not deducted.

VERBAL WARNING: The referee's verbal warning. Only one warning may be issued to each team per match.

VOLLEY SERVE: The most traditional way to serve, this is when the server releases the Pickleball ball with one hand and hits it before it is allowed to bounce.

New terms for 2021

Here are some of the newest Pickleball terms to be officially recognized in 2021:

EJECTION: When a player is prohibited from participating in a tournament by the Tournament Director due to unacceptable behavior.

MOMENTUM: A body in motion, after hitting the ball, remains in motion...Duh, really? Thanks, Isaac.

Plane of the net: The imaginary vertical planes that extend beyond the net system on all sides.

Profanity: Any words, phrases, or gestures that are considered too impolite to use around children or in polite company. Using a profanity may go against Pickleball etiquette!

Retirement: Even though Pickleball may be your retirement game of choice, you won't want to call a retirement during a match. If you do so, it means you have decided to stop the match and award the point to your opponent.

Hope to see YOU on the courts!

May your Pickleball adventures lead you to places of beauty.
Thanks for joining me in mine!

~ Patrick Smith
Lake Sebago, Maine

About the Author

Patrick W. Smith, born and raised in Washington State, now resides in Guilford, Connecticut and Frye Island, Maine. He is known by family and friends as a person who is a deep thinker with a great deal to share. His clever wit and ability to design and build stuff is inherited by his two adult daughters, Lucy and Jody, both powerful women in the world.

Patrick is a virtuoso percussionist/tympanist and musician. He has toured the world, performing with many artists and can be heard on numerous recordings. While living in Hong Kong, he was principal percussionist with the Hong Kong Philharmonic. In the Northeast region, he has worked extensively in all types of music and theater, from New Haven's Historic Shubert Theater to Broadway, and from The Royal Albert Hall in London to Lincoln Center and Carnegie Hall in New York City.

Mentoring musicians of all ages for over four decades, Patrick is now a Grammy Recognized and award-winning music educator. For his years of working with urban youth developing the next generations of great contemporary musicians, Patrick received Yale University's prestigious "Ellington Fellowship Award" from its founder, Professor Willie Ruff, Yale School of Music.

In addition, Patrick is also a Master level black belt instructor with Dillman Karate International. As a devoted student of the martial arts with nearly 60 years of training in numerous styles, he offers classes throughout New England and online.

In 2017, Patrick rediscovered Pickleball on the Frye Island courts with his wife Melinda who is a Certified Coach with the International Pickleball Teaching Professional Association and is passionate about the game. Melinda designs *Carpe Dink'em Pickleball Vacation Adventures* through *All Travel With Heart.*

She is creating community through Pickleball to serve as a vehicle for change, building connections and friendships throughout the world.

Patrick and Melinda both are Level One Certified practitioners of Kingian Nonviolence Reconciliation, bringing forth nonviolence as a way of life and spirit.

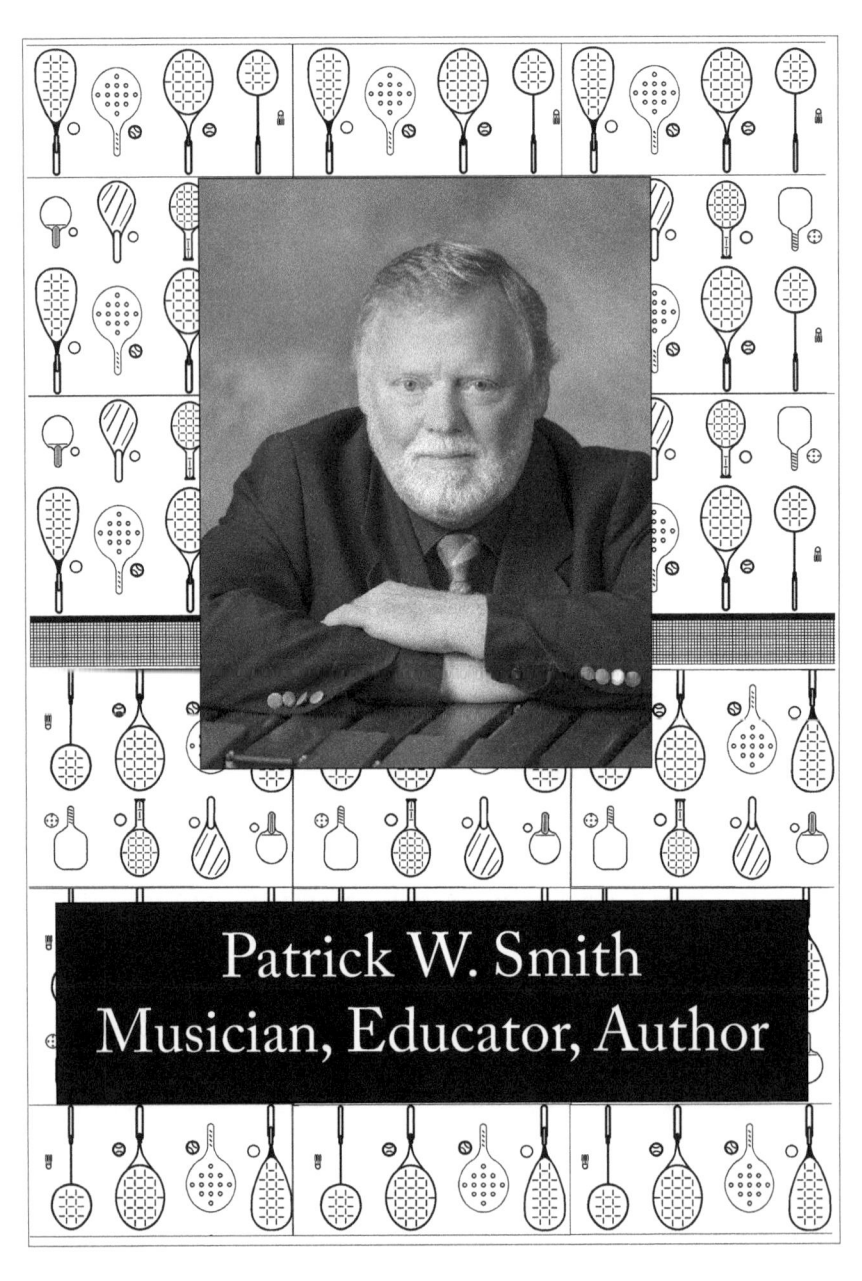

Patrick W. Smith
Musician, Educator, Author

Father John

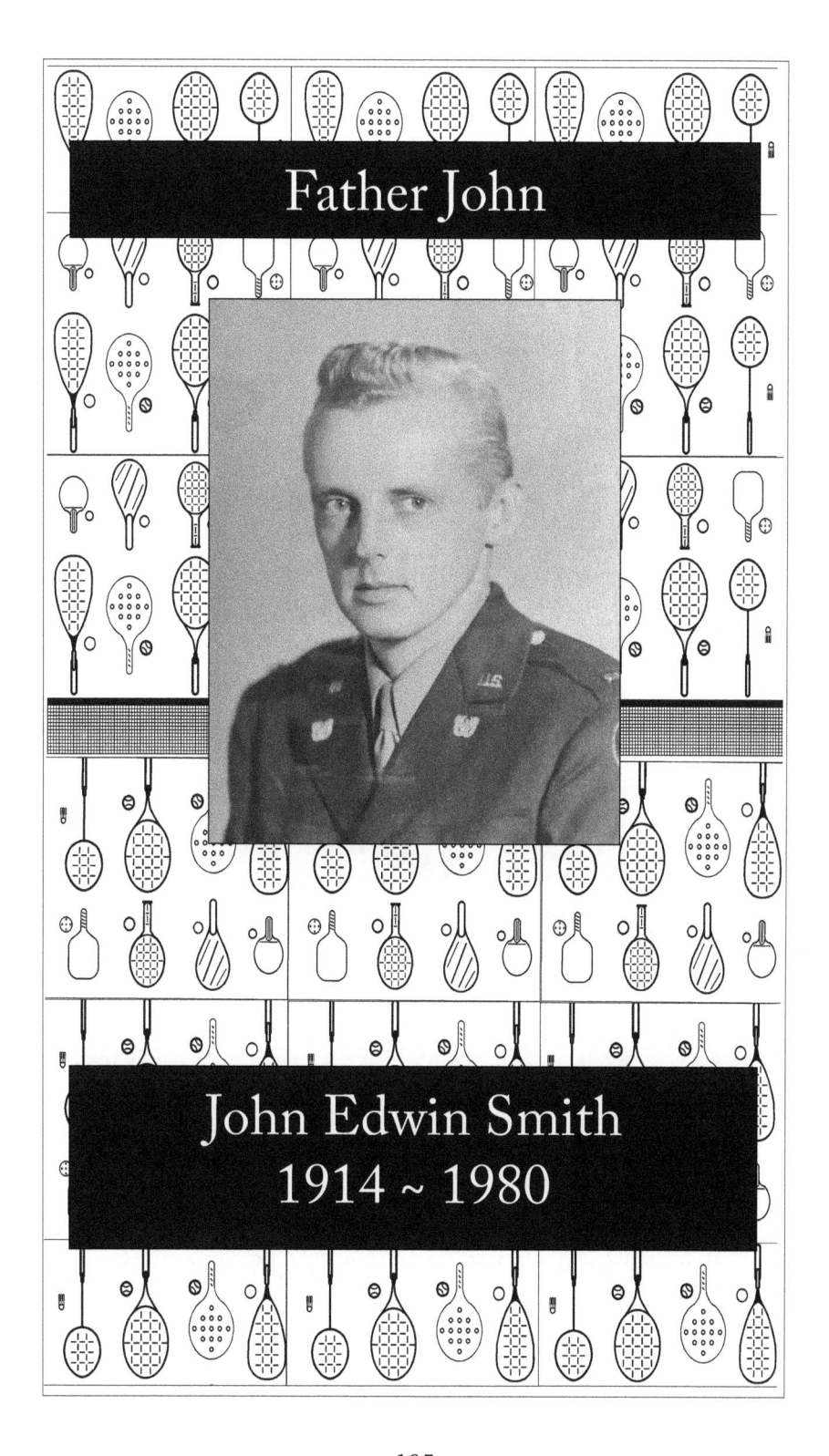

John Edwin Smith
1914 ~ 1980

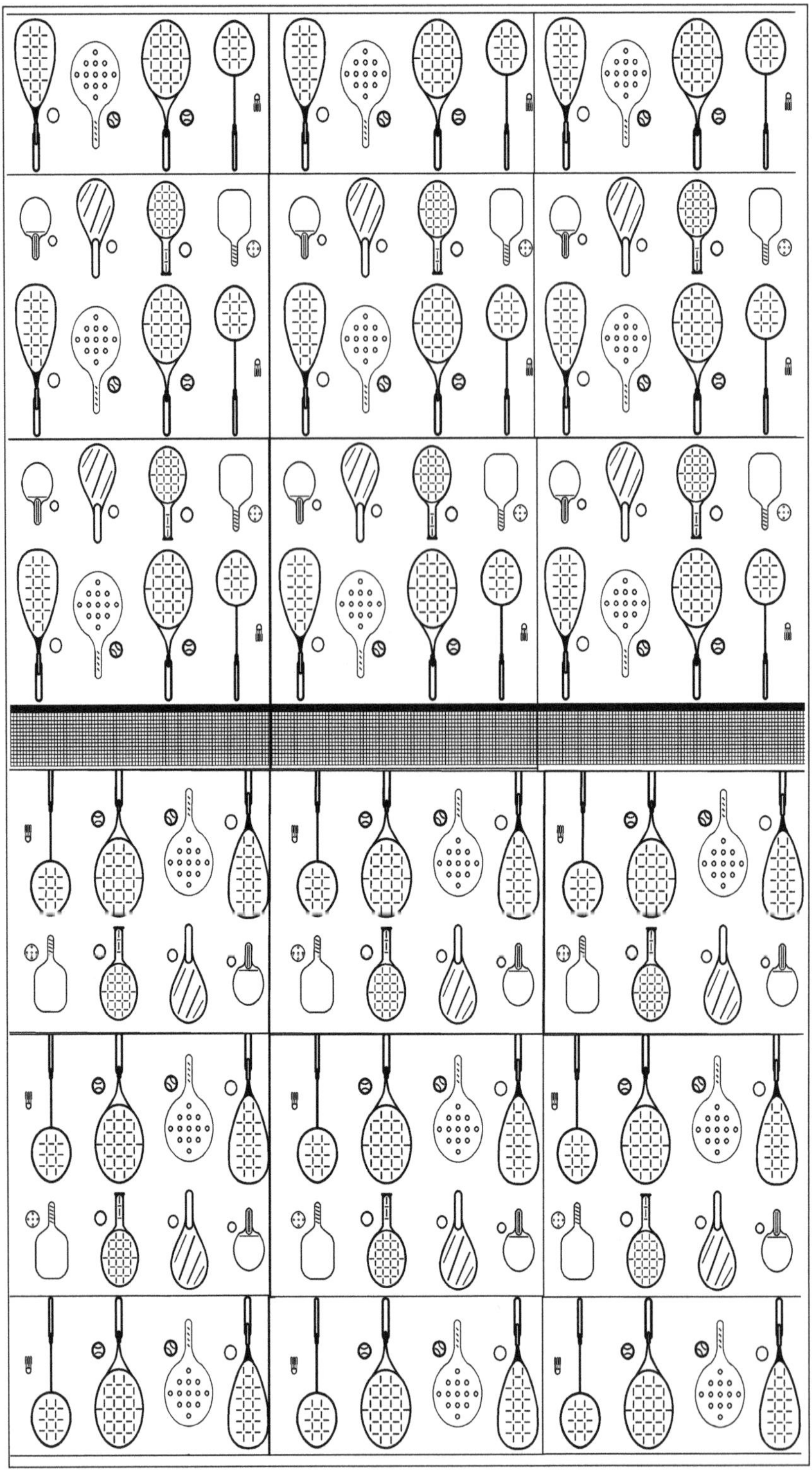

Photography, Image Credits, Permissions, and Acknowledgements

Cover Design - Book Designers - www.BookDesigners.com
Author Photograph - Harold Shapiro
Interior Design & Layout - YBPV
Landscape & Lake Sebago Images - @eye_of_ken
Ken Tabris photographer - used with permission
Derelict KALAKALA image used with consent - Sean Griffin
Shark Images/Lineart - FreePik.com
Seattle Historical Archives - Images used with permission
iStock Images: Cartoons, Drinks, Foods - licensed for print publishing
Museum of History & Industry MOHAI, Seattle, Washington
KALAKALA, Chief S'iahl- licensed for print publishing
Harper's Weekly - historical image 1874 - Public Domain
All Map Graphics - Patrick W. Smith
Player Action Photographs - Patrick W. Smith
Live Player Images permissions and waivers on file with YBPV
Special thanks to Sally Hill for technical support
& Shelley Sprague for additional culinary contributions

YBPV especially thanks
Maria Mortali
editor-in-chief
Master Chef & Baker, Food Artist Extraordinaire
for her Pickleball-Party
historical recipe research and testing

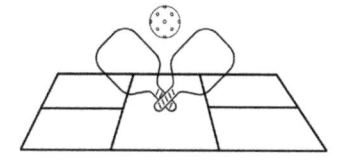

Fonts used in this manuscript
Noteworthy - Author's & Contributor Signatures
Brandon Grotesque - Chapter/Section Titles
Adobe Caslon Pro - Text Body
Big Caslon - Image Captions
Wingdings 3 - Graphics
This manuscript was designed and assembled by
YellowBird Publishing Ventures using
Adobe InDesign CC, Adobe Photoshop CC,
Adobe Bridge CC, Adobe Acrobat Pro 2017-2022

*A Parting Shot, after a good game
Peace on Lake Sebago, Maine*

CPSIA information can be obtained
at www.ICGtesting.com
Printed in the USA
BVHW011026120723
667127BV00009B/166